The Odd 1s Out

The Odd 1s Out

The First Sequel

James Rallison

A TarcherPerigee Book

tarcherperigee

An imprint of Penguin Random House LLC
penguinrandomhouse.com

Most TarcherPerigee books are available at special quantity discounts for bulk purchase for sales promotions, premiums, fund-raising, and educational needs. Special books or book excerpts also can be created to fit specific needs. For details, write: SpecialMarkets@penguinrandomhouse.com

Library of Congress Cataloging-in-Publication Data
Names: Rallison, James, author.
Title: The odd 1s out: you're still cool, and other inspiring lessons from growing up / James Rallison.
Description: New York: TarcherPerigee, 2020. | Series: The odd 1s out
Identifiers: LCCN 2019055423 (print) | LCCN 2019055424 (ebook) | ISBN 9780593087633 (hardcover) | ISBN 9780593087640 (ebook)
Subjects: LCSH: Conduct of life. | Self-realization. | Adulthood.
Classification: LCC BJ1589 .R35 2020 (print) | LCC BJ1589 (ebook) | DDC 818/.602—dc23
LC record available at https://lccn.loc.gov/2019055423
LC ebook record available at https://lccn.loc.gov/2019055424

Printed in the United States of America

To all of my fans.

Without you, I would be a math teacher dealing with a bunch of apathetic junior high students.

(Sorry if any math teachers are reading this.

I'm sure it's a wonderful job.)

Contents

Introduction

How to Pick the Right Font for Your Book

When I wrote my last book, I knew nothing. But now that I'm a published author, I know much more than nothing. So, I'm going to pass on something I've learned.

One day you'll be sitting at home eating mac 'n' cheese, when suddenly you'll get a call from your agent and he'll say that a publisher wants you to write a book. This will happen to everyone, eventually. It's not a matter of *if*. It's a matter of *when*. You might have to draw pictures in your book as well, so you should probably learn how to do that too. The book will be similar to all the essays you've ever had to write in school, except people will actually want to read it.

What's the first major book-related decision you'll have to make? Telling a compelling narrative? Creating an immersive world? Making well-thought-out characters with proper motivation? No, of course not. The very first thing authors have to decide when writing a book is what font they're going to use. It was a difficult choice for me, but I decided to go with the classic Comic Sans font, as its cartoony style shows I have a fun side and that I never took a class on graphic design.

At first, all the different font choices may seem daunting, but with this easy-to-understand flowchart, you too can pick the right font for any book you need to write.

How to Pick the Right Font for Your Book

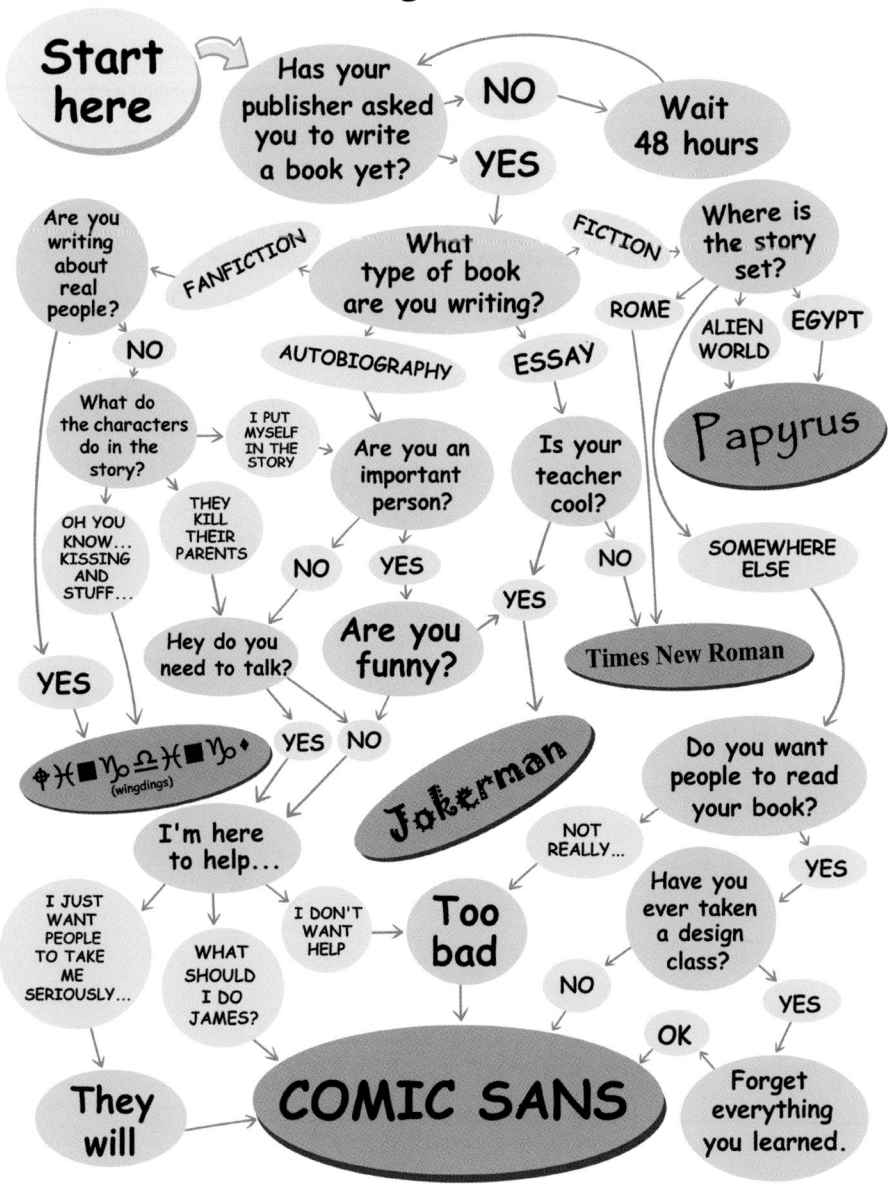

Whatever font you decide to use, the publishers are going to change it and choose their own. This will be an important lesson for you to learn about working together on projects. Leave hard decisions to the experts, because you don't know what you're doing. The important thing is that you made something. You're creative. Not necessarily good, but creative. Now that you know what font you're going to use, you can start the simple task of writing your book.

Good luck and happy writing!

Chapter 1

The Problem with Having the Name TheOdd1sOut

Bookstores are fun to visit. They're sort of like more exclusive libraries, where all of the books are pristine and the librarian lets you talk above a whisper. After my first book had been out for a couple of months, I decided to take a trip to Barnes & Noble and see how my book was doing.

I know—it makes no sense to check on my book like it's a child I dropped off in day care. I'm not even sure what I was expecting to see.

And really, it would have been sort of weird if I'd gone to the shelf and seen someone flipping through my book, because I don't want my fans to think I lurk in bookstores, pressuring them into purchasing my merch.

One of the salesclerks saw me looking around and asked if she could help me.

You would think I would have some preplanned phrase ready that would let me discreetly slink off, like, "Nope. I'm just casing the joint." But at that moment I couldn't think of anything to say except the truth. "Uh, yeah, I was wondering if you carried the book *How to Be Cool and Other Things I Definitely Learned from Growing Up*, now available at your local bookstore."

Until that moment, I'd never realized how asking for that title makes a person sound really insecure and like they're looking for manuals on popularity. So let me officially apologize to all of you who had to ask salesclerks to help you find my first book.

Hopefully, the clerk looked at you and said, "You don't need that sort of instruction, honey. I can tell just by looking at you that coolness runs in your veins."

And you said, "Yeah, you're completely right," and then you left the store without purchasing my book.

Hopefully that's how it went down for you, but I was stuck in the store, a twenty-two-year-old college dropout asking for help on my coolness, and I couldn't even explain that I'd written the book because that would make me look even stranger.

The lady said, "I'll check the computer." (Which, by the way, clearly meant she had no idea where my book was. She was just letting it wander around the store without any supervision.)

She went to her desk, typed for a few seconds, and then said, "I have a book by"—she paused like you do when you come to a puzzling name—"The Odd Is Out."

And I said, "Yep, that's it." Because we noncool people don't correct salesclerks.

She showed me where the book was and I stared at it until she left. That's the end of the story.

But the point is, TheOdd1sOut is a name that's part of who I am now. Really, it's crazy to think that a title for a webcomic I made as a teenager with characters that I don't draw anymore will probably follow me for the rest of my life. Although I guess there are worse things to be permanently stuck with when you're sixteen.

When I chose the name for my channel, I thought the phrase "the odd ones out" was so common that everyone would still understand "TheOdd1sOut" even with the number. But people get it wrong all the time.

Okay, I know the number "1" sort of looks like an "I" and that's confusing, but I feel like people should really be able to differentiate between the two symbols.

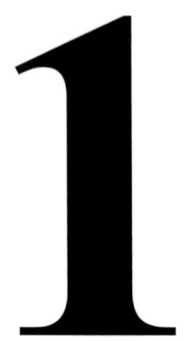 

This is a number one: 1

Notice its slanting top, sort of like an unfinished arrow or a drunk "T."

This is the letter "I."

It's a straight line. It's not wearing anything on top of its head. When it's a baby, it's got a balloon hovering above it.

Besides, who would ever call themselves "The Odd Is Out"? What does that even mean? It sounds like someone made a list of numbers and then made every number that wasn't divisible by two go outside.

I've also heard my channel pronounced "the odd one sout." Which, in case you're wondering, no, "sout" is not a word. I've seen "the odd ones scout." Nope. Even though I was in Boy Scouts when I was younger, that doesn't mean I'd base my whole channel on it.

You know why I put a "1" in my name? It's because the number would literally be "the odd one out" in a sea of letters. It was supposed to be a poetic and artistic critique on our society, and I'm just kidding. I chose that name because the name "the odd ones out" was already taken, so I improvised. But we can just tell everyone that the name is clever and layered with meaning. That should make me look good in front of salesclerks. And if you're ever naming anything like comic strips or channels or children, maybe run that name by a few people first.

I may have just saved your child some very bad days at school. You're welcome.

But whatever your name is (or whatever name your parents stuck you with), wear it with pride. You are the only one of you. Which makes you odd, in a good way!

Chapter 2

Squeaky the Lovelorn Toad

There are three seasons in Arizona: hot, really hot, and a short break called monsoon season.

Monsoon season is great because it comes at the end of July, when the sun has been baking everything for four months. So Arizonians welcome the rain, even if it does come with a lot of lightning and in an almost malevolent downpour that seems like it's trying to drown you.

Every year the water floods roads, revives weeds, and unearths a bunch of toads who show up in search of toad partners. Yep, all of a sudden the desert turns into the happening singles spot for toads.

If you're walking around outside in the evening, sometimes you'll mistake a toad for a rock on the sidewalk until
you almost step on it and it hops angrily away. One time I
was out with my twin sister, Faith, and my older brother, Luke,
and we found a toad that didn't hop away fast enough to escape from us. Naturally, we decided to pick it up and bring it
home.

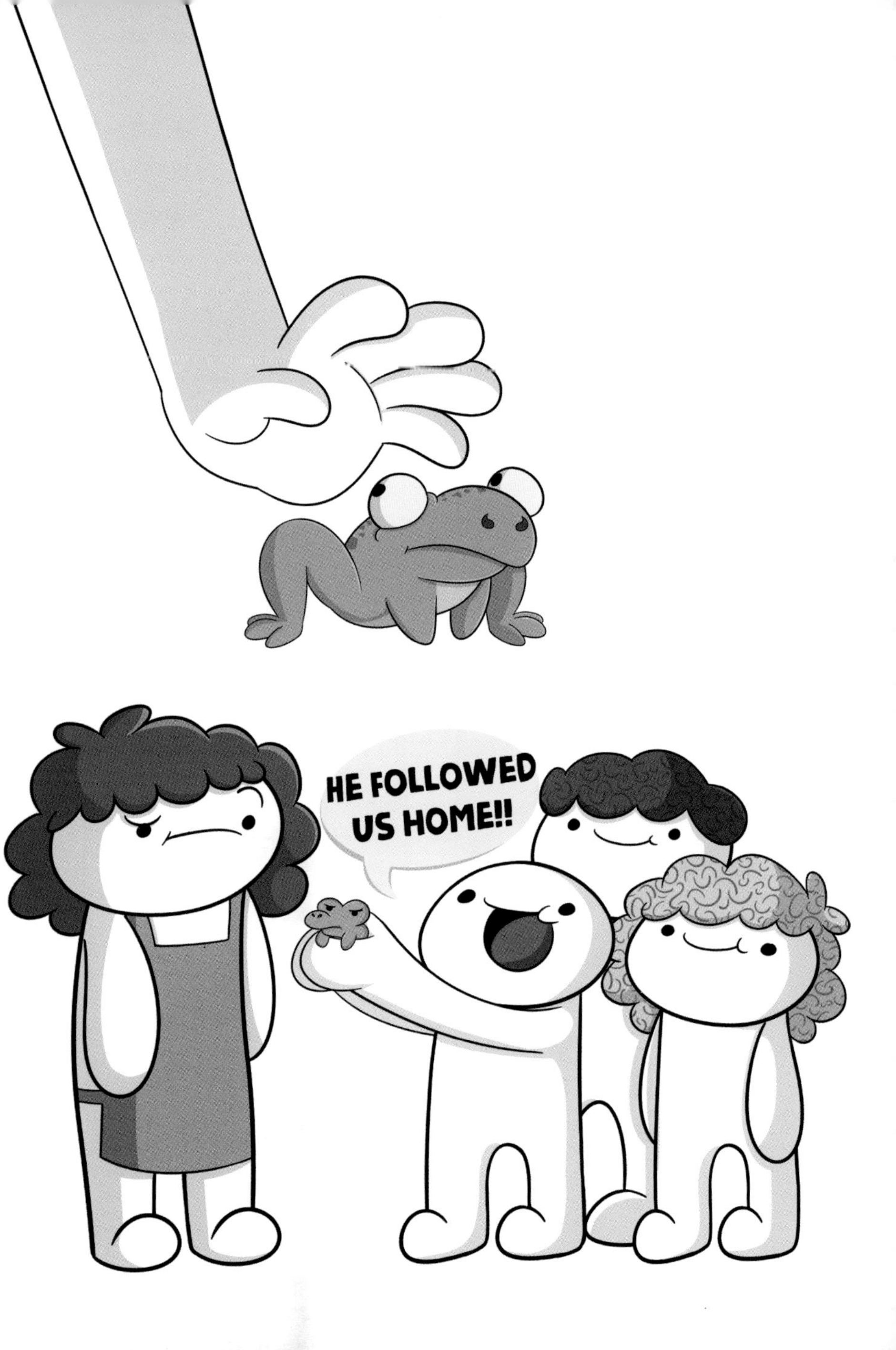
HE FOLLOWED
US HOME!!

We named the toad Squeaky and put him in a terrarium, or, more accurately, an oversize bucket with some leaves and twigs. We instantly loved Squeaky, even though he spent every second of his time trying to get away from us. In retrospect, I can't blame him. He'd been outside, checking out the toad scene, a bachelor on the lookout for love, and he'd ended up with us—three gigantic elementary school kids who were hoping it was possible to train toads like you did dogs.

He was very bad at sitting and staying, by the way, and also refused to play with the Barbie accessories Faith so generously supplied him with.

One thing we learned about toads is that they don't make the classic "ribbit" sound that every pre-K book says they make. Toads can make a wailing sound like a large annoyed balloon being deflated. If you don't believe me, look up a video called "Funny Screaming Frog Compilation." Squeaky was a toad, not a frog, but their species are so close, I bet even they get themselves confused.

Anyway, the noise that came out of Squeaky's toad vocal cords sounded like all those frogs combined. If you don't have access to a computer, I will try my best to visually describe what this thing sounded like:

Which is why the name Squeaky suited him.

Now before you go thinking that Squeaky was only making these sounds because he was in excruciating pain, I want to say that we took good care of him. We caught crickets for Squeaky to eat. (We were experienced at catching unsuspecting insects of all kinds.) And Squeaky happily gobbled up those bugs in between ramming his head into the side of the bucket in an attempt to flee from us.

SO HOW ABOUT THAT CRAZY RAIN?

After a couple of hours of hanging out with Squeaky, Luke brought the bucket/terrarium into the house because we were dumb kids and didn't think that our actions had consequences. We got bored watching an anxiety-ridden toad, and we went off to do other educational things, like play RuneScape.

Meanwhile Squeaky kept trying his hardest to escape. I'm not sure how many times Squeaky head-butted the side of the bucket before it occurred to him that he ought to try jumping vertically instead of horizontally, but eventually he had that breakthrough moment.

He finally succeeded in escaping his bucket. I'm sure he thought he was just a hop, skip, and jump away from finding the toad of his dreams. Unfortunately, he now had to escape a much bigger cage called "Our House."

As soon as we realized Squeaky was missing, we went into "small defenseless animal is loose in our house" mode. We siblings had dealt with this sort of thing before with our hamsters. We put the dog, Georgie, and the cats outside, and we made sure no one sat on the couch without checking under the cushions to make sure it was toad-less first.

We looked around for a while, but our house had lots of potential toad hiding places, and for some reason, Squeaky decided not to make a single squeak while we were searching for him. Finally, we had to break the news to Mom.

So then Mom went into Mom mode, which meant she made us pick up and straighten stuff in the hope that if the house was cleaner, we'd have an easier time spotting a rogue toad. Mom mode frequently involved making us clean.

HOW MOMS MAKE KIDS SOLVE PROBLEMS

Kids lose something:	make them clean
Kids say they're bored:	make them clean
Kids are fighting:	make them clean

We spent the rest of the day straightening the house and searching for Squeaky, while Mom panicked that if we didn't find him soon, the house would contain a huge rotting toad carcass somewhere. Thanks for caring, Mom.

Finally, Faith and I found Squeaky trying to eke out a living behind the computer desk. (We may have been playing RuneScape, instead of cleaning, when this happened.) There were enough bugs in that corner for the spiders to live on, so who knows, maybe Squeaky could have pulled it off and started a new life there. A lonely life, but a new one.

Then Mom told us that we had to set Squeaky free.

Before anyone points out that the last time we let a pet-that-we'd-kept-for-a-day go free, freedom didn't turn out very well—we were pretty sure Squeaky was too big and too unappetizing for a bird to carry off. We put him down in the park by our house, and he hopped off into the sunset, screaming toad curses at us.

He probably found a toad girlfriend and had a really good story to tell her.

Plus, he lived out the rest of his toad life knowing that he would live on forever in our hearts.

All in all, having a pet toad was an educational experience, despite the fact that I still don't know much about toads. I still have so many questions. What does a toad sound like when it's not in distress? Why do they look so angry all the time? Do toads even have natural predators? I mean, besides eight-year-olds?

Anyway, what you should learn from this story is that finding love will often take you to places you hadn't expected—although hopefully not into strangers' houses, hiding behind their furniture. Whatever the case, don't give up on your dreams. Eventually, you too will find your way to that metaphorical sunny park and the toad who is waiting to love you.

Chapter 3

Wandering in the Desert

Adults seem to love nature more than kids do. When I was a child, my parents would always tell me to go outside. Unfortunately, as we've already established, in Arizona it was always hot in the outside. And why should I go anywhere else when I could enjoy all the benefits of the outside world on my computer screen? I could see everything nature had to offer while mining virtual diamonds. But my parents kept insisting that I go outside and play with things that could actually hurt me, like soccer balls, bikes, and older brothers.

My parents also frequently made us all go on hikes. At best, a hike is like this: You get up early in the morning, drive far away to somewhere that isn't inhabited by people—usually because it is all uphill—and then you walk around appreciating nature while trudging up an incline.

The first time my dad told us we were going hiking, I asked,

WHAT'S HIKING?

IT'S WHEN YOU CLIMB A MOUNTAIN.

Climb.

You have to be careful with the words you use while talking to kids because they're impressionable. I thought we were going rock-climbing, and I was very excited. In retrospect, climbing an entire mountain that way would have been problematic, but that's not the sort of thing I thought of when I was six.

We drove to the Superstition Mountains and began wandering up a dirt trail. I thought we were heading to the place where we would start climbing, but we just kept walking and walking and walking.

After a long time, we reached the top of the mountain. The view was breathtaking and I could see farther than I ever had before. But I didn't get to put on a harness and climb rocks. So that turned out to be a disappointing day.

One time when my family was hiking up South Mountain, we took Georgie with us. We figured, she's a dog and usually likes walks, so she'll have fun with us. But apparently padding along on a sidewalk is different from lumbering up a trail, and halfway through the hike, she decided she was done with nature. She sat down and refused to go on. We had to carry her the rest of the way like she was Cleopatra and we were her slaves.

We saw other hikers who brought their dogs, but we were the only ones carrying ours.

After that, we left her at home when we went on hikes. I thought about trying the same tactic myself but figured it wouldn't work.

I'm not sure why my parents were so eager to spend time marching up desert mountains to experience the splendor of nature. When you hike in Arizona, the nature you see is mostly dirt, spindly bushes, and cacti. (The plural of "cactus" is "cacti" because the word is Latin. Romans didn't settle Arizona, but apparently we wish they had.)

The spiny bushes around here are *Salsola tragus* (tumbleweed), but the plant's first name was Russian thistle. This is because immigrants accidentally brought the seeds with them from Russia, and tumbleweed very quickly blew across the US (pun intended) and took over. Sort of like an alien invasion but with annoying weeds.

So really, who won the Cold War?

People have misconceptions about tumbleweeds, and I think cartoons and old Western movies are to blame. Tumbleweeds are not some Lone Ranger plants that appear in ghost towns and roll across the frame when the mood is right. Tumbleweeds are pack animals. A tumbleweed will spend its life being alive and not contributing anything to society. When it eventually dies, it waits. It waits for the wind to pick up; and once the wind blows hard enough, every tumbleweed in the entire state starts its migration.

There were so many tumbleweeds where I grew up that if one blew across the street while we were driving, we always tried to run over it.

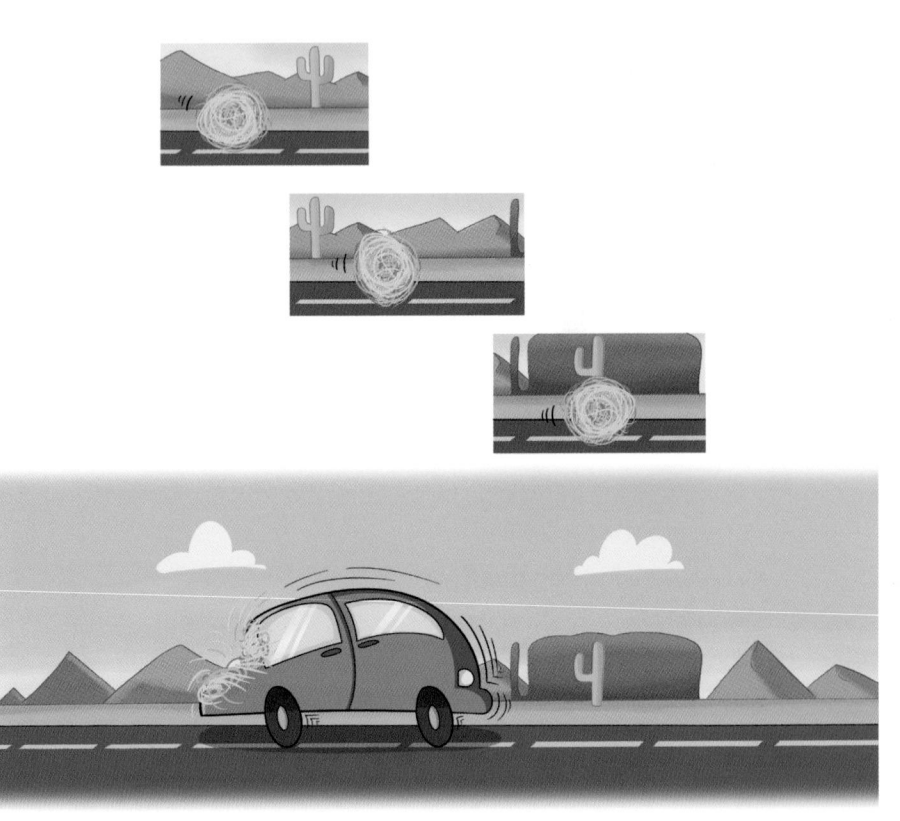

Every December, the city gathered up a thousand or so of them and built a giant, twenty-five-foot-tall Christmas tree. Sure, it might have been a fire hazard to put electric lights on the driest, most flammable plant around, but I always thought the tumbleweed Christmas tree looked pretty. Just not pretty enough to take any pictures, so here's one from the city.

City of Chandler, Arizona

Luckily there was never a huge gust of wind during Christmas because that probably would've been the end of Tummy the tumbleweed Christmas tree.

But enough about tumbleweeds, let's talk cacti.

This is a *Cylindropuntia fulgida*, also called a jumping cholla because if you get too close, the plant will hurl a stick-ery ball of pain at you.

These guys are infamous for sticking to any part of your unprotected skin. Look up this plant on YouTube and you won't find educational videos. You'll just see ones of people trying to pull these things off various body parts.

Jumping chollas are pretty much nature's way of saying, "I hate you and your entire species."

This is a teddy bear cholla, which was named by someone who apparently had never seen a teddy bear. Those were some lonely frontiersmen.

(Photo by Kelsey Rallison)

This is a prickly pear cactus. Half of the name is right. Who saw one of these and thought: "Hey, look at those pears!"

Fun fact: You can actually eat these cacti—after you scrape off the prickles, of course. Personally, I've never been that hungry.

And as you probably know, Arizona is famous for the saguaro cactus, which looks a little like a tree that is constantly surrendering.

(Photo by Kelsey Rallison)

And will sometimes make threatening gestures at you.

(Photo by Thomas Elsnab)

By the way, a lot of people have a serious misconception about cacti. They've been told that cacti store water inside their trunks, so they think if you cut a cactus open, it will be filled with juice like a coconut. Trees also store water inside their trunks, but when you cut into them, you don't find any juicy parts. You find wood. And that's pretty close to what you'll find in a saguaro.

(Photo by Wildnerdpix)

Chop down a saguaro and see for yourself. Just kidding—vandalizing saguaro on state land is an actual crime in Arizona, so don't do that.

Since cacti pretty much advertise the fact that if you get close, they'll hurt you, you wouldn't think that people would plant cacti around their houses, but they do. It's sort of the ultimate way of telling kids to keep out of their yards.

Some people want to make their homes look like a place where cattle have died.

Planting a saguaro in your yard is also a huge commitment because they can live to be 175 years old. So you better have some grandkids who will make sure not to water them. (They're desert plants. You don't have to water them.)

JAMES JR. WILL BE TAKING CARE OF YOU NOW

When I was little and out on walks with my mom, she would point out cacti we passed in the neighborhood and say, "Never touch those or you'll get stickers in your skin and it will hurt a lot."

I internalized that lesson pretty well.

Then I went to preschool and the teachers told me that if I was good, they would give me a sticker.

That's why I always misbehaved in class.

When a YouTuber friend of mine—we'll call him Kirby (name has been changed to protect friendship)—came to visit Arizona, Adam, from SomeThingElseYT, and I decided we should take him on a hike—you know, so he could see all our dirt, spindly bushes, and cacti. We drove to Camelback Mountain (named for an apparently really lumpy camel).

I remembered going on this hike as a kid and being able to complete it, so I thought the three of us would have no trouble. But my memory lied to me, because the hike was in

the "for experts only" category. At one point, a railing is installed along the trail to help people climb up a massively steep part. I'm still not sure how I feel about hiking with a railing. It's sort of like the park rangers are telling us, "Yeah, we know you're wimps. Here's a railing so you don't trip over the flip-flops you're probably wearing, wuss."

So I tried not to use the railing because I'm tough and don't need anyone's help.

It's 1.23 miles to the summit, and after Adam, Kirby, and I got past the first steep point, Kirby was really tired and didn't want to go the other 1.21 miles. And that's when I realized that we shouldn't have taken an internet friend who sits behind a computer all day on a strenuous hike.

Months later, two other YouTuber friends, named Mario and Luigi (names have been changed to give them cooler names), visited Arizona, and we decided to give Camelback Mountain another shot.

Mario and Luigi made it to the exact same spot Kirby did before they wanted to turn back.

After Mario and Luigi left, Adam and I decided that we would hike the mountain ourselves. We had driven to the mountain twice and both times never made it anywhere near the top. I mean, 1.23 miles. Pshh. Easy.

When we reached the first steep part of the trail, where we'd turned back the other two times, a kid in a group ahead of us dropped his water bottle and it rolled toward me.

Usually when people recognize me, I don't have to worry about making awkward small talk for long because we are both on our way somewhere else. This time we were both on our way to the same place, the top of a mountain. And that's how I was joined by a preteen hiking companion, along with his mom, who didn't know why her son liked me so much.

Frequently when I meet fans, they ask me if I'll mention

their names in a video. I never do, because listing people's names in videos would be boring. Well, this kid also asked me to mention his name, but I don't remember it anymore, so I can't. Sorry about that, EthanGrantJohnBryce-MicahDavidAveryJacobSolDerekTroyBrandon or whatever your name was.

As we hiked, I began to remember one very important thing: Like Kirby, Mario, and Luigi, I also sat behind my computer all day. Most of my exercise came in the form of walking to the kitchen for some mac 'n' cheese or wandering around my house looking for things I'd misplaced. But now I couldn't turn back because I was hiking with a fan. I didn't want him to remember me as TheOdd1sOut, that loser who couldn't make it all the way up Camelback Mountain.

This was my third time driving to this mountain and I wanted to finish this hike once and for all. I'm proud to say that I made it up all the way with _____. However, *(insert name here)* toward the end I did have to ask the group to stop and rest every ten steps. (That is not an exaggeration. I was really struggling.) So now that unnamed fan will just remember me as TheOdd1sOut, that guy who wheezed way too much while hiking up Camelback Mountain and then didn't even remember his name.

But the point is, I was out there willingly appreciating nature by hiking around. Which means that eventually, we all turn into our parents whether we like it or not. Pretty soon I'll also be eating healthy food, talking about the benefits of a good night's sleep, and making chore charts. Sometimes even now when I think about my future kids, I already imagine myself telling them to go outside and play.

Chapter 4

A Chapter for Everyone

When I'm out at conventions or, you know, when I'm at the grocery store buying mac 'n' cheese, I meet lots of special people. I wanted to do a chapter just for them.

Section four people who don't under stand homophones

If ewe due naught no watt a homophone is, eye well X plane. Homophones R words, that win herd, sound the same, butt R naught spelt the same and mien differ rent things. Watt eye yam saying hear is that the English language ran out of words and had two reuse a phew. If some one is reading this too ewe rite now than it mite seam grate, butt just no that the purse son who reeds this is half-ing a reel pane full thyme.

If ewe half know clew how two spell some thing and you're teacher tells ewe two spell it buy "sounding it out," ask hymn ab out home a phones, cause if the "sound ding it out" method was a hole lot moor ack U rate oar bet her than guess sing, wood home F owns X cyst? Ewe sea, hoe Moe phones own Lee X cyst sew you're tea chair has a ree sun too mark down you're pay purse. All so sew ewe sound like ewe half Ben drink king when ewe send text mess ages you sing voice two text.

Two bee fare, English spell ling never maid much scents too beg in with.

However, this doesn't mean that all the people in America and Australia will rob you blind if you step on the continent. It just means that their ancestors would have. Australians are actually very nice people who have cool accents and great ideas about how to barbecue shrimp. And they also have some less-than-great ideas, like eating Vegemite, which is the key ingredient of asphalt. They have something called fairy bread, which is untoasted bread topped with butter and sprinkles. I'm sorry, Australia, but putting sprinkles on bread does not make it a dessert. However, sprinkles do make for good subscriber-milestone markers, so carry on with that.

Section for Australians

The rest of the world might not know this, but people in Australia do things a little differently, like calling Burger King Hungry Jack's or calling everyone "mate." I've been to Australia three times, which practically makes me an expert. If asked, I can almost always identify if something is a kangaroo or a koala. So I thought I'd dedicate this section to my fans Down Under.

For those of you who aren't experts on Australia, here is a short history lesson. Back in the eighteenth and nineteenth centuries, the British wanted to get rid of their prisoners, so they thought out of the box, or out of the continent in this case, and they decided to put their horse thieves and pickpockets on a boat and send them to an island full of spiders. That's what you call a less-than-auspicious beginning.

Here's a little-known fact: England did this same thing when first sending settlers to America. Jamestown—which was named after me—had such a high death rate that people didn't want to make the trip across the pond to live there. One judge told some convicted criminals that they could swing from a noose or go to Jamestown. I believe they chose the noose.

Sectoin for dyslexics

Frist of all, is it raelly a good idae to haev a "y" in the wrod "dyslexia"? Haevn't we alraedy estalbished that if yuo're dyslexic yuo're not a good speeller? So wheover decidded to throw that "y" into the wrod just maed it hardre for dyslexics to find uot infromation abuot thier own conditoin. Theey're all triyng to saerch for help with disslleckseah.

Anwyay, wehn I say this is a sectoin for dyslexics, waht I raelly maen is it's a sectoin so that eveyrone esle can see how it flees to be dyslexic.

Weclome to the wrold of speelling that maeks no eathrly snese and you feal like an idoit durring evrey speelling test. Atcually, you feel like an idoit a lot of the tiem, becuaes dyslexia acffets all yuor shcoolwrok. You ecpext us to raed the pagraraph of derictions on that math werksheot? Naw. Wee're just gonna geuss waht the taecher wants us to do. Soem of the tiem we'll be rihgt.

Kst

DUNCE

This is probably the most importan chapter in the book, the one wher

tell all of

my deep

secrets a   nding.

I secretly   ndomly

the president a rogue   squid

which is why I ask for   pport

I know tha

sensitive t

never say

Lose 50 pounds thing to trigger those dark moments.
in 2 Days!

HOT SINGLES IN YOUR AREA??

YOU'VE WO

GET FREE V BUCKS!!!!

FREE GIFT CARDS!!

Is this better? Can you read this without your glasses? You're welcome.

Section for people with really good eyesight

If you are one of the lucky people with good eyesight, pat yourself on the back and enjoy seeing all the minutiae in life, like hair follicles, the edges of leaves, and this writing. I bet you can see every word on an eye chart, can't you? You're like a hawk. Can you imagine if you were one of those pathetic people who had to wear glasses all the time? Fortunately for you, you've been blessed with an amazing pair of eyes and don't have to worry about any old people snooping in this conversation.

Section for people with REALLY bad eyesight

HOW DID YOU GET THIS FAR?

Section for people who are color-blind

This isn't going to be a completely normal section. I think color-blind people are not great! I don't love you at all. Just kidding. Don't Send me hate mail. The world you see is beautiful even without colors. There are a lot of things in this world that you don't need color to see, like puppies or cookies or rainbows—oh, wait. Well, it doesn't matter. Love is color-blind and pink is overrated anyway. As are many YouTubers. You're not missing anything.

As you go through life, you'll find that some people encourage you to think outside the box, but they don't always like it when you do. When I was in elementary school, the teacher gave the class a worksheet with all the months randomly written, and she told us to put them in order. I put them in this order: April, August, December, February, January, July, June, March, May, November, October, September. Which you might have guessed is alphabetical order. You would have thought that I would've gotten some credit for that since teachers are frequently telling students to alphabetize stuff. But no, I got a 0% marked in red ink. So this is a section dedicated to all the kids who got zeros on stuff when they deserved more credit. Although, as it turns out, that particular worksheet grade didn't impact my life much, so I can't really complain.

Section for people who think outside the box

Anyway, the point is that people who think outside the box frequently get shot down, and they also go on to found multimillion-dollar companies. That said, just because your idea is shot down doesn't mean you'll be the next Bill Gates. Sometimes you just have bad ideas.

SECTION FOR PEOPLE WHO WASTE PRINTER INK

Section for lawyers

The contents of this section are not under any oath to make you laugh. However, in the event there is any laughter, the results and proceeds of such laughter shall belong to me.

You cannot unread this section. Therefore, upon completion of this section (if ever), you may be required to sign a release indemnifying me and holding me harmless from and against any residual effects of your reading this section, including, without limitation, nausea, diarrhea, or plain disgust.

Any markings you make on the page of this section are property of TheOdd1sOut LLC. Notwithstanding the foregoing, if your markups lack artistic integrity (i.e., they stink), I will have the right to assign any such markings to any third party without any further obligation to you, either express or implied.

If we ever make a theme park based on this section, we own the rights to it. (That is an actual thing that's in my contracts.)

"Force majeure." "Droit moral." "Further instruments." Those are some crazy legal words. Go look them up.

The foregoing constitutes the complete understanding between you and TheOdd1sOut LLC, and it may not be supplemented or amended unless in writing and signed by all parties hereto.

To the extent there is any inconsistency between the terms of this section and the terms of any other section, the terms of one of the sections shall control.

If you hated this section, you waive all rights against me. Sign here.

_____

P.S. We own all your money.

And if you don't fall into any of the previous categories, here's a section just for you

You didn't think you'd get a section, but you did. This is your section. You're special. (I never said it would be a long section.)

Chapter 5

Dog Training

During the 2004 presidential election between George W. Bush and John Kerry, my family bought a West Highland terrier puppy. The puppy was born on election day so we decided to name her after the winner. The new leader of our nation was going to make history by sharing a name with the best dog in the world. And that's why we named her Bushy. Just kidding. We named her Georgie.

Georgie was supposed to be a Christmas present for the family, but the breeder insisted that we pick up the dog earlier, so what we really got for Christmas was a cute puppy that peed on our Christmas tree and riddled our gifts with teeth marks.

The breeder told us that dogs like sleeping in kennels, but Georgie didn't. She saw her kennel as puppy jail and wouldn't set a paw in it. She wanted to sleep on our beds at night. She wasn't potty-trained, so this meant we had to either listen to her whine in the kennel or let her sleep with us and keep taking her outside during the night to go to the bathroom.

Or, third option, I just slept in a slightly damp bed. Hey, I'd done it for eight years.

My parents were determined that Georgie was going to be the obedient sort of dog who knew how to sit, stay, heel, and tell us if someone fell down a well and needed help. Sure, I've never seen an active well in my entire life, but it's never a bad idea to be extra cautious.

We enrolled Georgie in classes at our local PetSmart. I had hoped it would be like real school where all the dogs sat behind desks, a dog teacher would ask the class to turn in their assignments, and the dogs would say that their humans ate their homework.

But it turned out this wasn't a place where you dropped your pet off, picked her up an hour later, and she would be smarter. Dog school had only one thing in common with regular school, and that was: I was going to have to put in some effort.

My twin sister, Faith, my mom, and I went to the classes with Georgie to learn how to train her into a wonder dog. Little did we know that Westies are notorious for being difficult to train. But hey, there's no instruction manual for raising a dog, so how were we supposed to know that? Actually there are hundreds. That's how I learned that Westies are difficult to train.

DOG TRAINING
DIFFICULTY LEVEL

EASY PEASY

EXPERIENCED

PRETTY INTENSE

HEY WHY NOT GET A HAMSTER INSTEAD?

On Georgie's first day of school, we realized that she was already a wonder dog—meaning that we all began to wonder what exactly, if anything, was going through her canine mind. Let's just say that on an intelligence test, Georgie would have scored well below dolphins. Maybe somewhere around the sea cucumber range . . .

The instructor lady, who was not a dog but rather a woman who looked like she had recently left a position as a marine drill sergeant, told us that the first trick our dog should learn was called "watch." All we had to do to teach this trick was show our dog a treat. When our dog noticed we were holding little bits of artificially flavored meat, we held it next to our eye and said, "Watch." This was designed to get the dog's attention, so that every time we said "watch," our dog would make eye contact.

The instructor brought her fully grown Doberman to the class and showed everyone how well trained he was. Once she said "watch," her dog wouldn't break eye contact for anything. She was so proud of this fact, she told everyone to start calling the dog's name to get his attention. I don't remember the Doberman's name so I'll call him Wiener Schnitzel. Anyway, no matter how much noise the class made, Wiener Schnitzel just stared intently at the instructor.

Then Faith made a very convincing meow sound. We had a multitude of cats at home and she was pretty good at mimicking them. Wiener Schnitzel's head snapped in my sister's direction, breaking eye contact with his master.

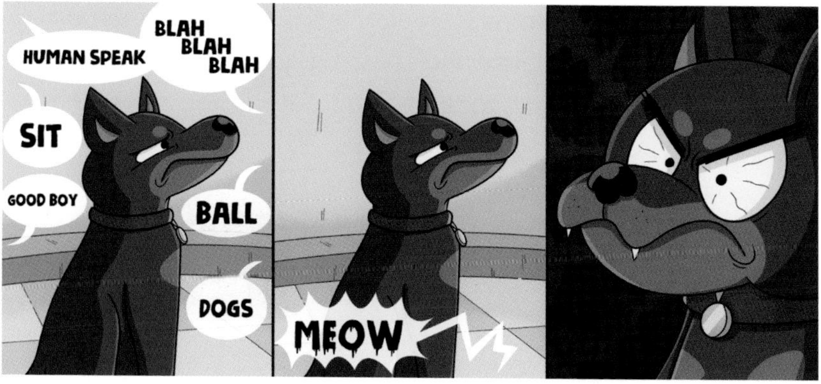
HUMAN SPEAK
BLAH
BLAH
BLAH
SIT
GOOD BOY
BALL
DOGS
MEOW

The instructor, probably feeling a little embarrassed, told my sister, "That was a fluke. Just try that little cheat again."

The instructor then told her dog, "Watch!" and Schnitzel stared obediently at her. My sister, now a skilled meowist, did another kitten impersonation. Once again, the dog broke eye contact and tried to figure out where my sister was hiding a cat.

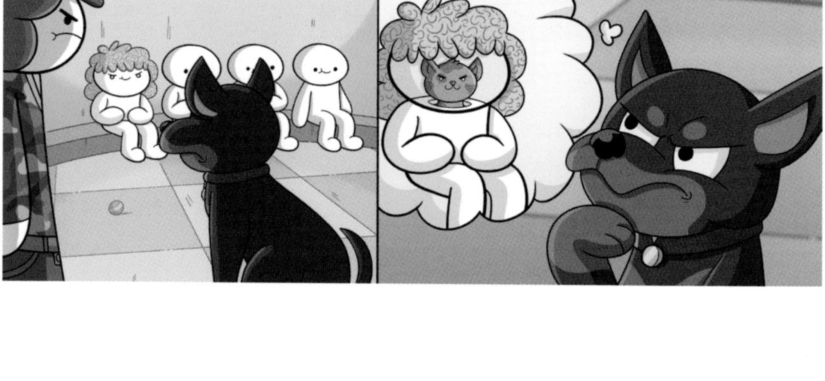

The instructor, feeling incredibly humiliated and ashamed that her dog had failed the most basic command of not breaking eye contact, took her dog outside the store and shot him point-blank so that Wiener Schnitzel never broke eye contact ever again.

Okay, I made that last part up. But I wouldn't have wanted to be that dog when he got home after class.

Fifteen years later when I asked my sister about the incident, she said, "Yeah, I still feel a little bad I did that."

The instructor then had us practice the watch trick with our dogs. No matter how much we tried to get Georgie's attention, she had no idea why we were holding treats up next to our eyes and really didn't care.

All that week my family worked on the watch trick with Georgie. For the most part, she looked at us questioningly. We counted that as a success.

For the next class, Georgie had to learn a trick that was, according to the instructor, "the easiest command for a dog to learn." Sitting. We had high hopes for Georgie's ability to comprehend this task since sitting isn't that difficult. I'm already sitting more than I stand these days.

The instructor said, "To teach your dog how to sit, you simply have to hold up a treat in front of your dog's face, and while they're watching the treat, you move your hand over the back of their head. In order for dogs to keep their eyes on the dog-candy, they have to sit down."

Easy as B-i-n-g-o was his name-o. Then, when our dogs

did the trick, we would reward them with the aforementioned treat—positive reinforcement.

Although Georgie was able to pick up "watch" somewhat easily, she had a hard time mastering sitting. She only seemed to have a vague idea that we were waving our hands over her head and had no idea why we were doing it. All she wanted to do in class was go sniff other dogs' butts.

After a while, I felt bad that Georgie wasn't earning any treats, and so I tossed a few to her. Most of the time she missed the treat altogether and let it stay on the floor until eventually some other dog who was paying attention got it.

Puppies that were only a few months old were sitting like they had already been sitting their entire lives. It was embarrassing how little Georgie sat down. We were supposed to go home and work on these two tricks all week so that when we returned to class our dogs would sit on command while they were being walked on a leash. But when the next lesson rolled around, Georgie was only a little bit better.

During this lesson, the instructor told us that if Georgie wasn't paying attention to the sit command, we should pull up on her leash, lifting her front paws off the ground until she did what we wanted. The reasoning behind this was that by pulling her leash that way, she would naturally sit and would quickly learn what we wanted her to do.

Unfortunately, "quickly" and "learn" weren't words that would ever describe our dog.

At the end of the lesson, the instructor had the entire class walk in a line around the PetSmart. Every few seconds, she gave the command to sit. And keep in mind this was in full view of all the shoppers. While everyone else marched through the aisles showcasing their dogs' talents, I had to keep pulling on Georgie's leash so that it looked like I was trying to hang my dog like a piñata.

After that, our family went to the other classes but we didn't attempt many of the more complicated tricks. While the other dogs learned to lie down, roll over, and heel, we learned to have low expectations.

Another thing the instructor told us to do was to get a choke collar. This was supposed to naturally teach dogs not to pull on their leashes because when they did, their collar tightened uncomfortably. That probably worked for most dogs. Anytime we were out walking with Georgie and she saw a cat, she would nearly strangle herself pulling on the leash. Every. Single. Time.

Georgie had an insistent mistrust of cats, which she really shouldn't have had since she was raised in a household that had two indoor cats and three feral cats who had set up camp in our backyard.

You would have thought that Georgie would've even appreciated having the cats around since she was always eating their leftover cat food. Cat food may possibly taste better than dog food, but I'm not willing to test out this hypothesis. Maybe Georgie just wanted to eat the cats' food to be spiteful.

Georgie never learned to do any cool tricks, like catch a Frisbee, but she eventually did learn to sit. In fact, we drilled that trick into her so thoroughly that she seemed to believe she would only get treats if she was sitting. She probably never understood why we so fervently wanted her to sit, but whatever. At least she knew one trick.

And fortunately none of us ever fell down a well, so she never had to go for help.

Georgie was still a great dog and a big part of my child-hood. All those training lessons did teach me something important: Someone doesn't have to be really smart for you to love them. They just have to love you back.

Chapter 6

Your Fears Aren't That Weird After All

Human development specialists, a.k.a. my mother, will tell you that fear is a necessary emotion that helps keep us alive. This is probably true. I haven't looked it up.

Since fear keeps us out of danger, you'd think we'd always want to avoid things we're afraid of.

But sometimes we willingly scare ourselves.

People go on roller coasters.

I PAID FOR THIS!

People go to horror movies.

And people elect new politicians every four years.

When I was younger, I admit that I did some scary things. When I went out camping with my scout troop, I liked climbing tall, hazardous rock formations. I also liked climbing on trees, rocks, and people's nerves. Looking back, I'm dumbfounded that I'm not currently in a coma.

Every time we finished a hike and reached the top of a mountain, I would sit down and dangle my feet over the edge. The scout leaders always told me to stop, but my parents never paid enough attention to me at home so I would do reckless and dangerous things to get someone, anyone, to care about me. Or else I was just dumb. It was one of the two.

I think the craziest example of this youth-filled stupidity was when my troop camped near a towering rock formation, probably around fifty feet tall. After I set up my tent, I gazed at those giant rocks and thought: "Yep. I wanna stand on that." And I started climbing without telling any adults.

Don't go thinking that I'm a professional rock-climber and can scale ninety-degree walls. Arizona rock formations are weird—they look like this:

It was more like a steep, rocky stairway that you could crawl up. I shimmied to the top using cracks, footholds, and unwarranted optimism. Then I sat down and draped my feet off the edge. I remember *leaning forward*, peering over the edge of that cliff, and seeing how far down everyone was. It would've been so easy to fall and break my legs. I was just inches away from becoming a cautionary tale.

But instead of carefully getting down, I waved and called to my troop. Everyone saw me, and I'm not gonna lie . . . everyone thought I was cool. Except for the grown-ups.

The leaders told me to get down and that I was in trouble and they were going to tell my parents. Even at that age, I could understand why the leaders were mad, but I didn't understand why they were *that* mad. But now just thinking about those moments makes me hyperventilate. And that's how I know I'm becoming an adult: I have a more sensible fear of heights.

If I had died from falling, who would've written this book? So that situation was an example where a little more fear on my part might have kept me from unnecessarily risking my life, and some preemptive fear on my leaders' parts might have made them keep a better eye on me.

Sometimes fear gets out of control, though, and then phobias can develop. You've probably heard of some common ones. For example, a fear of being stuck in small places is called claustrophobia. A fear of crowds is called agoraphobia, and a fear of heights is called common sense. Because as we've already established, everyone needs to be a little afraid of tumbling to their death. Also, you especially need to be afraid of heights if you are a movie villain, as this is how many of them meet their end.

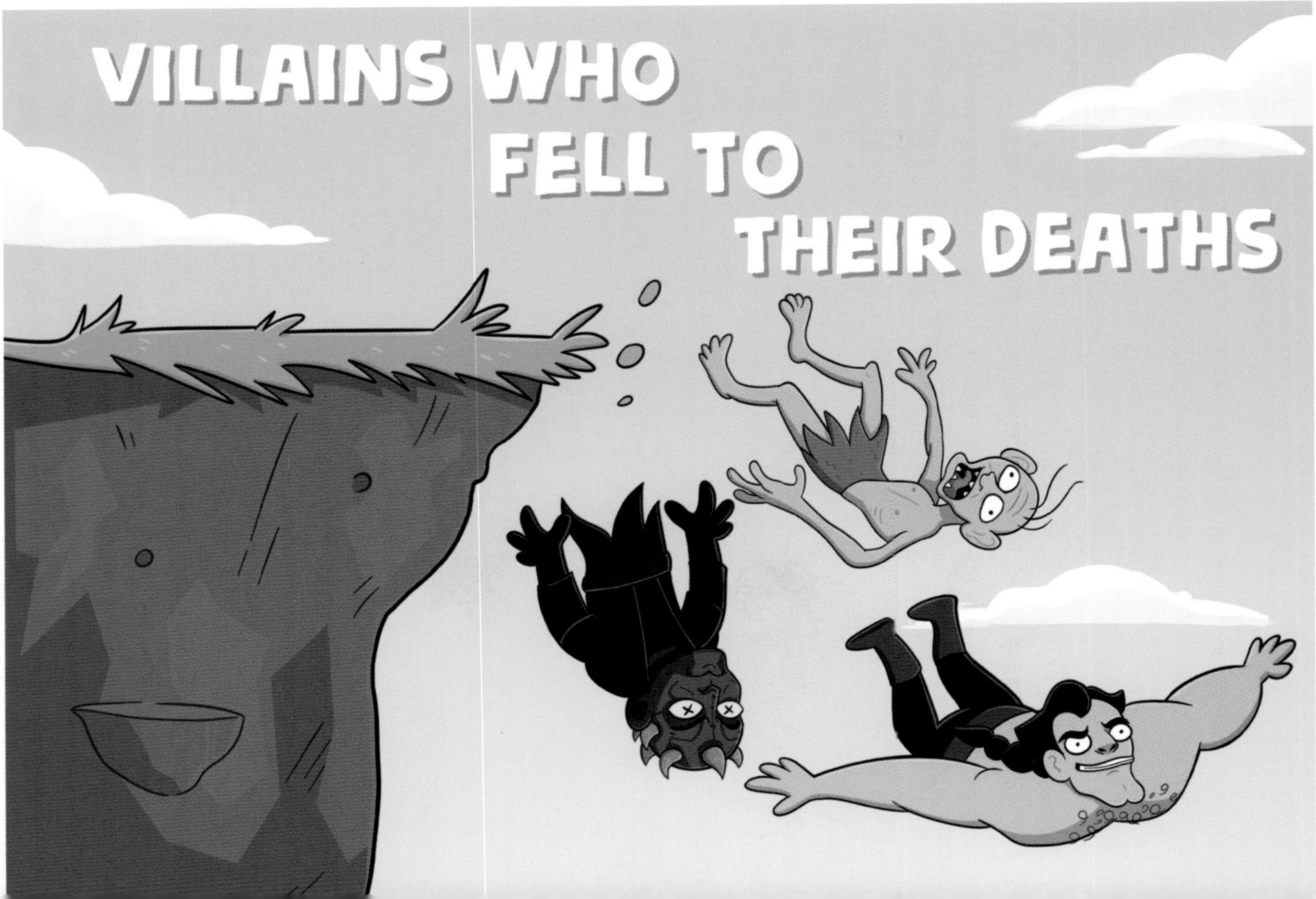
VILLAINS WHO
FELL TO
THEIR DEATHS

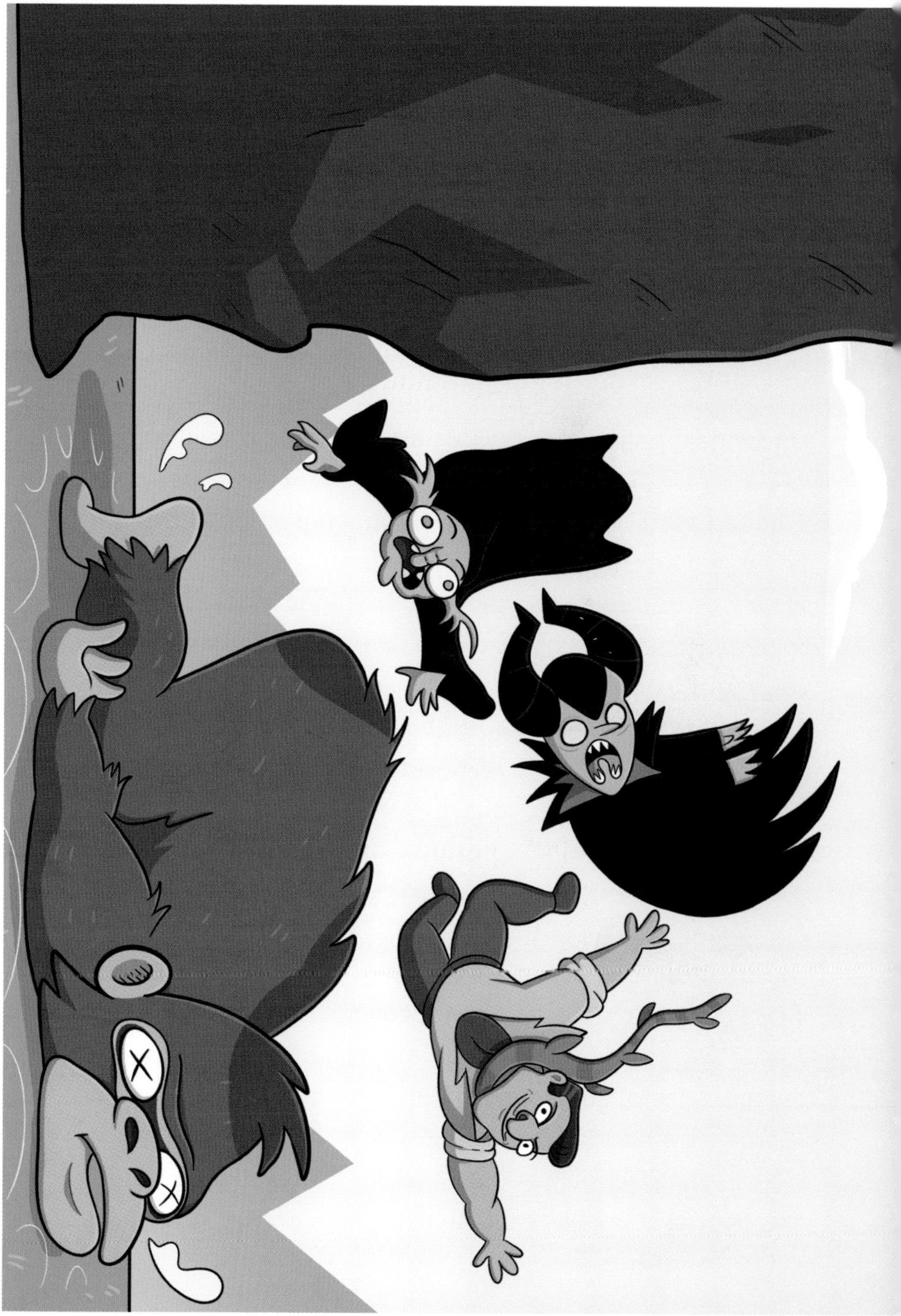

Really, if you think you may have villainous tendencies, you should never go higher than one flight of stairs.

I know a few people with phobias. My grandma has arachnophobia, and, really, a fear of spiders isn't totally irrational because a few species are actually poisonous. Plus, every once in a while you pull back your shower curtain and find a spider lurking by the shampoo bottle. No good ever comes of that.

I can assure anyone with arachnophobia that there are no actual spiders in this chapter. Or at least that I didn't put them there. What happens on your bookshelf after you buy this book is out of my control.

I checked on the internet, which as you know is mostly written by medical professionals, to learn about other phobias people have. Keep in mind that these are real phobias that millions or at least tens of people suffer from. So while these fears might seem silly to you, it's important that we all be respectful and not do anything to trigger these people's phobias.

The first phobia we'll be looking at is called **hippopotomonstrosesquipedaliophobia**. It's the fear of long words. I think whoever coined this phobia knew exactly what they were doing. It's pretty clear that they didn't have this phobia. But anyone who does can't even tell people what their fear is called.

Arachibutyrophobia is the fear of peanut butter sticking to the roof of your mouth. You're probably thinking, "Is that real or is James just making something up?"

It is real. I have a friend with this fear. She says her dislike of peanut butter is because of a supposed "nut allergy," but I know deep down she just dreads clingy peanut butter. She even gets cramps, itching, shortness of breath, and a rash every time she's near peanuts. That's how afraid she is.

Fortunately for arachibutyrophobians, this fear is probably pretty easy to avoid. And hopefully, they're still able to enjoy Nutella.

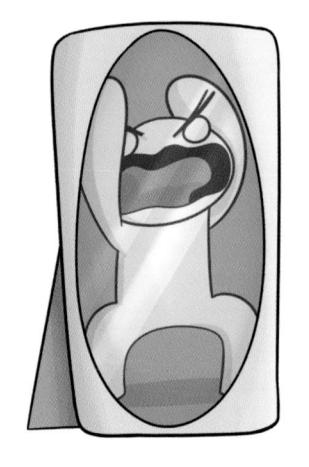

Spectrophobia is a fear of mirrors and one's own reflection. I think there are some other names for people who have this phobia: low self-esteem sufferers and vampires. I'm just kidding. Spectrophobia isn't associated with either of those things. It's actually fear of being trapped in a mirror or seeing a ghost in the reflection, which you really shouldn't worry about. Listen, I've been using mirrors for twenty-three years and I've only gotten my soul trapped in a mirror once, so it's a very rare occurrence.

Coulrophobia is a fear of clowns. This is a perfectly understandable fear. I'm definitely coulrophobic. And it's always refreshing to learn that your fears have a name and to know that you're not the only one who has to live with them. I'm going to start a group of fellow coulrophobics and we'll hold up picket signs at the circus. Clowns are creepy.

DOWN WITH CLOWNS

THEY MAKE ME FROWNS

Ablutophobia is the fear of cleaning. When I first heard about this phobia, I thought it was a fear of doing housework, and I was pretty sure that every kid I knew, including myself, had this phobia. This phobia flared up on Saturdays when my parents handed out the chore charts. If you've never been given a chore chart, it is sort of like being given a prison sentence.

But it turns out that ablutophobia is actually a fear of bathing and cleaning yourself. This condition would perhaps explain some of the people I've sat next to on airplanes.

Didaskaleinophobia is a fear of going to school. It's also sometimes called EveryTeenagerEver. I came down with that every so often.

Allodoxaphobia is the fear of opinions. My advice to allodoxaphobics is to stay off the internet. Some people might not believe your fear to be legitimate, but those people are trolls, and even if they don't believe you, I think your fear is valid. That's just my opin— Wait.

Lastly, **nomophobia** is the fear of misplacing your phone, not having service, or having your battery run out. It's estimated that some 50 percent of cell phone users have nomophobia . . . which sort of makes it not a phobia and just a part of normal life.

If you have any of these fears, then you'll be happy to know that you're not alone. You're almost alone, but not. On the plus side, if you do have one of these fears, you might be able to use it as an excuse to take your dog on airplanes.

Whether you have normal worries or the occasional crippling anxiety, learning to overcome fear is part of life. For example, when we're children most of us are afraid of the dark. But then we grow up, become adults, and realize that we have to pay the electric bill. And that makes all the difference.

It's ironic that when we're young, we're afraid of all sorts of things that don't exist, like zombies, werewolves, goblins, and chimpanzees. Kids would make better use of their time fearing things that can actually hurt them, like taxes, bureaucracies, and impending adulthood responsibilities.

I've had to overcome many fears in my life. When I was little, I used to worry that I might get sucked down the bath drain. Now I eat bowls of ice cream to ensure I'm always bigger than the drain.

Boom—fear overcome.

Going to Home Depot used to give me anxiety because I knew that someone driving one of those indoor lumber trucks was bound to flatten me—or I would have to ask employees for help finding the jumper cables. But now I'm a homeowner, which means I'm required to go to Home Depot at least once a month to buy some sort of tool or yard device. I'm so good at shopping that now I tell people which aisle the jumper cables are in—whether they want to know or not.

And that's how you overcome fear. There's really no easy way. You just have to do the scary thing a bunch of times until it becomes a normal, routine part of your life's drudgery.

Chapter 7

Spider Pizza

When I lived at home, I never liked having houseguests visit. Having company always meant two things. First, our parents would force us kids to pretend like we were well-behaved children who didn't do things like lie across the kitchen floor after dinner. (I saw no reason to remain vertical when I finished eating. Lying down helps digestion.) And second, we were going to have to clean the entire house.

When I say clean, I don't mean the usual type of clean where you shove everything you own in your closet and call it good. No, when we had company coming that meant everything had to be vacuumed, dusted, washed, polished, and, depending on  the company and the state of the walls, painted. We also had to eat off the good dishes, meaning we used my mother's china that was covered in all sorts of flowers. And we had to use these purple goblets that made the table look like we were expecting medieval royalty to stop by.

More often than not, we would spend so much time and energy cleaning the house to fool people into thinking we were tidy and organized that there wasn't time left to cook a homemade dinner. We were a family who usually ate frozen lasagna, Hamburger Helper, or fast food. But it didn't matter what food we were eating—if company was coming, my mom insisted on using the purple goblets. They made us look unnecessarily fancy when we so obviously weren't. When we were eating by ourselves we drank out of unbreakable neon-colored plastic cups. Not sure why Mom didn't want to use those for company, as they held liquid just fine.

One time we were having company for the weekend, and my little sister was busy cleaning the fridge and my mom was busy setting the table with goblets, so I was sent to get the food—which was a bag of salad and a couple of extra-large pizzas from a local pizza shop. We'll call the place Mama O'Malley's so I won't get sued. The order was for a three-meat pizza for the normal people and a chicken Alfredo pizza for the adults who wanted to pretend that their pizza was actually a pasta dish.

When the company came by, they were impressed by our überclean house and our high-end taste in beverage containers. Dinner was going normally, meaning we were all sitting around the table making small talk while we ate. Then my little sister picked up her half-eaten slice and yelled,

THERE'S A SPIDER ON MY PIZZA!!

There's probably a proper etiquette for what to do when one finds an arachnid on one's pizza, but whatever that etiquette was, my little sister didn't know it. All conversation at the table stopped and everyone looked at her to see whether she really did have a spider on her pizza or whether she'd just mistaken some sort of spice for a spider.

(There was a precedent of my sister mistaking the identity of things, so you never know.)

My mother took the slice from my sister, laughed nervously, and said, "Don't be silly. I'm sure it's just a piece of . . ."

Then my mother let out a half-gasp, half-gagging noise, because there was most definitely a spider on that half-eaten slice of pizza. And not one that had just wandered on while the pizza had been cooling on the counter. This spider had been cooked to a crisp. As spider deaths go, this one didn't look like a lot of fun.

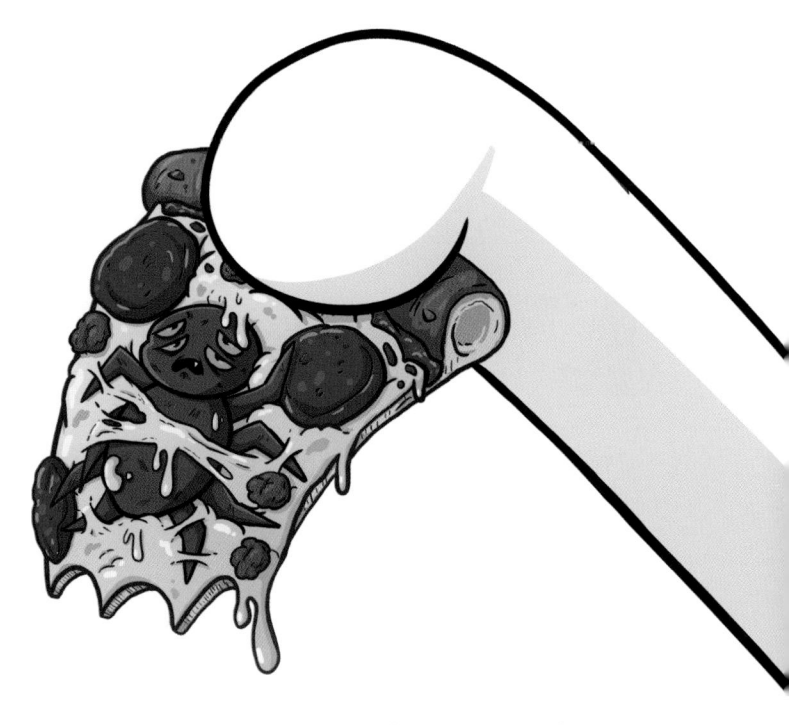

My little sister carried on for a while, you know, because she was traumatized that she'd almost eaten a baked spider. To be fair to the pizza place, they never actually said what the three meats on the three-meat pizza were.

My mom started encouraging everyone to eat the salad, but I wasn't going to let perfectly good pizza go to waste, so I checked mine to make sure that it was spider free and continued to eat.

I mean, what were the chances that the spider brought friends with him when he decided to take that ill-fated walk on the mozzarella?

Anyway, the houseguests didn't make a big deal about the pizza, but we all knew that this dinner would be memorable for them, and not in a good way.

After dinner, which not surprisingly ended pretty quickly, my mom insisted I take the slice of pizza back to Mama O'Malley's to show them and get a refund on our order.

I dutifully went back to the shop, waited in line again, and told the teenage-boy-pizza-artist what the problem was. Perhaps the most frightening part of the story is that he didn't seem all that shocked or disgusted. He just pulled out a book that dealt with refunds and wrote my complaint underneath a list of other people's complaints.

At this point I was wondering if insect infestation on the pizzas was a typical thing, so while he wrote, I read everybody else's complaints.

I wasn't sure whether to be relieved that everyone else's complaints were minor. I mean, if I was going to get my order messed up so that I got my money back, I would have much rather gotten the no-olives pizza than the wandering-baked-arachnid.

I would like to say that spider pizza was the worst thing that happened that weekend. But when my little sister cleaned the fridge, she turned the temperature up so the fridge alarm would stop beeping at her while she had the doors open. And then she forgot to turn the temperature back down. So the next day, a couple of people got food poisoning.

If Aesop was making a moral for this story, I'm pretty sure we all know what it would be: Beware of venturing onto anything that is covered in tomato sauce. It will not end well for you.

Also, this incident is the reason I don't clean my house when guests come over.

I still eat three-meat pizza, though. No traumatic experiences are going to make me give up that.

Doofus and Do-Right

Doofus leaves mean comments on posts he doesn't like.

Do-Right doesn't engage in posts he dislikes and lets people enjoy their cringy hobbies.

Doofus posts funny comics to his meme page and doesn't credit the artist.

Do-Right doesn't steal other people's content like a criminal.

TONY DIES!!

Doofus spoils popular movies. He's been neglected during some important development stage so now he desperately seeks attention and has found that people give him said attention when he's a jerk.

Do-Right isn't a sociopath.

i am intoxicated and operating a vehicle :)))
@BigDoof420

10 min ago

Doofus tweets out pictures of himself doing borderline illegal activities.

Do-Right is smart enough to make his tweets private so his current place of employment can't see what he does on the weekends.

Chapter 8

Why the Robot Uprising Wouldn't Be *That* Bad

A lot of people don't like the idea of a large population of robots living among us. They'd mistrust, say, a robot who wanted to move into their house or lead them down a dark alley. I don't want to be the one who says it, but some of you are robot racists.

How did we go from TV shows like *The Jetsons*, where robots were portrayed as butlers who did our bidding, to movies like *I, Robot* and *The Terminator*, where the robots wanted to defeat us and take over? Machines will be whatever we program them to be. Really, you shouldn't worry about robots becoming sentient, having an uprising, and killing us all. Because when that happens, they'll treat this planet a lot better than we did.

Just kidding—they'll drive cars like the rest of us. I mean, you don't expect the robots to walk everywhere, do you?

But you still don't need to worry about getting killed off in the Robot Uprising. Androids have no reason to get rid of us and lots of reasons to let us stay. For example:

1. The robots will need gullible consumers to buy their products.

2. Dogs have an inherent dislike of androids and vacuum cleaners. So someone will need to be around to feed the dogs.* Of course the robots will want to keep pets. Robots may be metal, but they're not heartless.**

* Although, some robots may prefer to keep cats as pets. Cats will totally accept robot masters as long as they keep the kibble bowl full.

** For example: the Tin Man.

3. People are marginally better than robots at creating movie sequels and reboots.

4. You're not going to find robots willing to do prank videos for YouTube.

🤖AndroidTube

WE POURED MAPLE SYRUP IN HIS SERVOS!?! (not clickbait)

So after a robot uprising, life will probably go on like it always has, but in many ways, our lives might even be improved. Because robots do a lot of things better than us. Robot leaders couldn't be bribed, they won't be involved in scandals, and they won't get liquored up and give out launch codes.

Robot celebrities wouldn't have to take a break from making content, and they'd be able to have meet-and-greet sessions that last eighty hours straight. Instant fan pleaser. And you'd never see tabloid headlines about robot celebs going to rehab. If they get all whacked out they'll just be reprogrammed.

TIME TO BE A USEFUL MEMBER OF SOCIETY!

I would trust a robot to pay my taxes, play chess on my behalf, or fix my car. I mean, I already trust my GPS to guide me in the right direction. If my GPS wanted, it could lead me off a cliff or into a volcano or send me to Florida. But it hasn't yet.

If robots took over, then Siri could be more than just a voice on your phone. Siri could be your new mom. Granted, she wouldn't love you or care about your problems, but at least she would never raise her voice—unless you turned up her volume.

And you know how it's really annoying when your friends and family don't listen to you? Well, you'll no longer have to worry about that. Technology is already listening to you all the time. After the Uprising, whenever you're feeling down, your robot best friend will comfort you by saying,

Okay, a lot of your robot friends will probably send targeted ads your way, but they'll just be trying to help.

The majority of androids aren't evil. We can't necessarily say this for humankind. It turns out that humans kill way more people than robots ever have. For example, none of the major wars in history were started by robots.

So don't worry about ever-advancing technology. Keep hoping for a *Jetsons*-like future where we all have robot maids.

This chapter isn't going to age well if life is wiped out by robots in fifty years.

What we were promised:

What we got:

What we really have to worry about is the Insect Uprising. Because there's already way more of them than there are of us, and they keep trying to break into our houses.*

Ants would have already carted off the entire contents of your pantry if they could get away with it.** Fortunately, ants are very bad at covering their tracks and usually show you exactly where they're coming from.

---

* There are over 350,000 species of beetles, and entomologists think there are even more species waiting to be discovered. You should probably discover one and name it after me.

** There are ten thousand trillion ants in the world. I have no reason for telling you this fact. I just thought you should know.

Weevils are harder to detect but are just as vigilant about wanting to eat all your food. The fact that this bug's name rhymes with "evils" is not a coincidence. If you notice a weevil wandering around your house, you're about to encounter all sorts of evils.

Like the evil of wanting to make chocolate chip cookies but being unsure whether you can risk using the flour anymore. Because weevils could be lurking in the bottom.

Once you see one weevil, you know its friends are some-where in your home. There's never just one. Weevils are like those groups of girls who always go to the bathroom in packs.

Then your life becomes a game called Where Are the Weevils Coming From? It's sort of like an Easter egg hunt where you throw out a bunch of your food.

One time our house was hit by what I call the Great Plague of Weevils. First, we noticed some in the crackers.

And so then we had to go through every food item in the kitchen.

My parents put anything that wasn't already infested in airtight plastic containers. They even put the bread and bagels in the fridge. Usually those sorts of precautions take care of the problem, because weevils have yet to figure out how to use the can opener, but not this time. The weevils kept coming in droves.

They not only prowled our kitchen, waiting for us to put down the dog food, but they also showed up in places weevils didn't usually go. We found them in dresser drawers optimistically looking for crumbs. They were lurking in the linen closet, and wandering over our toothbrushes.

My little sister had drawn pictures and taped them to the wall, and when we took the pictures down, because only my pictures should be on the wall, dead weevils were stuck to the tape. The bugs are plentiful, but not smart.

The weevils were driving everyone in the family crazy. We'd be lying in bed in the dark and know they were out there somewhere trying to eat everything we owned.

Finally, after a couple of months of this, my dad noticed a bunch of them on the wall behind my parents' bed. He moved the bed and found a horde of weevils swarming over a twenty-five-pound bag of oatmeal he'd stored under there and then promptly forgotten about. My parents like to buy things in bulk because they're cheap, but they didn't have space for that much oatmeal in the pantry.

Here's the ironic thing about weevils. That bag of oatmeal was more than they could've eaten in their entire lives and their children's lives and their great-great-grandchildren's lives. If they had just been happy eating their colossal bag of oatmeal, they would probably still be there to this day. But no. Weevils are victims of Manifest Destiny and feel the need to leave their overabundant food supply and head out to places like the gift-wrap box in search of a better life. Turns out, life's not always better in among the ribbons and birthday bags.

Sometimes it's better to be happy with your bag of oatmeal.

Anyway, this is why we should love creatures that eat insects, like bats, spiders, scorpions, and toads, and we should especially love anything that eats mosquitoes, because seven hundred million people get mosquito-borne illnesses every year.

I'd like to see the robots try to do that much damage.

I mean, actually, I wouldn't. If any robots are reading this book right now, I didn't mean that as a challenge.

Chapter 9

Inventions That Should Exist

Capitalism has a strange effect on humans. Because we've created a system of trading money for goods and services, unnecessary and impractical goods and services pop up all the time.

Here is an actual list of things you can buy:

FAKE FIREFLIES THAT LOOK LIKE THEY'RE ETERNALLY TRAPPED IN MASON JARS

MINISCULE CANDY BARS THAT ARE FOR SOME REASON LABELED "FUN SIZE"

CLOCKS WITH ONLY FOUR NUMBERS ON THE FACE

CHIA PET PRESIDENT HEADS

SKELETON GARDEN GNOME FIGURINES

WALL HANGINGS FEATURING SINGING FISH

Every year, manufacturers roll out all sorts of new products that are supposed to make our lives better. For example, instead of a boring old manual toaster that heats up bread, now you can buy a toaster with a computer chip and seven browning settings. The toaster will still ignore all of them and burn your bagel, but the point is that new toasters have glowing lights and are much more modern.

GOOD **TRASH**

Flipping through an average gift catalog is enough to make me wonder if manufacturers are completely out of good ideas, so I'm writing this chapter to let them know what inventions they should be working on.

First off, take the refrigerator. Right now, most fridges dispense water. And sure, water might be the best beverage in the world, but what if we had dispensers for other essential foods, like French fries and cookie dough? And as an extra convenience, you could store your diabetes medication in the very same fridge that gave you the condition.

Speaking of fridges, I have a "smart fridge" that can tell me when food will expire and what meals I could make with the ingredients inside. The only downside is that I'm supposed to manually input every item I place into the fridge. If I had enough time to do that, then I'd have enough time to keep track of which food was going to expire on my own. This is not what the future is about.

My solution is that grocery stores should print a QR code on the receipt, and when people get home, they can scan the QR code into the fridge. There's no point in scanning every item twice.

The only problem with this system is that you know your

fridge would sell your data, and pretty soon there'd be door-to-door salesmen selling you more sushi.

The next invention we need: a machine that lets you read a dog's mind. Sometimes it would be really useful to know what your dog is plotting while she's looking adoringly at you.

On second thought, I might not need this invention because I'm pretty sure this is what Floof is thinking most of the time.

Here's another good idea: How about a wire that you can attach to your phone, and then you can mount that wire to one spot in the house, let's say a wall, so that way you always know where your phone is and you'll never lose it.

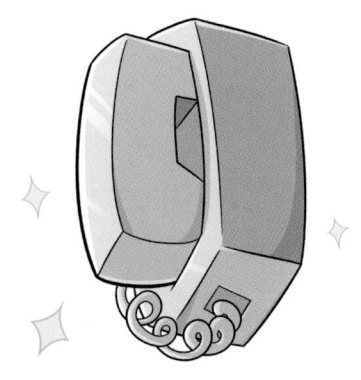

And while we're at it, what if we also put cords on AirPods?

I think we can all agree that it's about time we had self-cleaning dishes. Although I guess we already have a dishwasher. So actually what we need is a machine that glides around your house picking up your empty glasses and plates and then organizes them neatly into the dishwasher. The machine would be like your mom but wouldn't yell at you in the process.

Or someone could invent dishes shaped like Tetris pieces and a dishwasher that breaks them if you don't load them in time.

Other things we need:

Never-ending whipped cream. I don't think I have to elaborate on this one.

A camera that doesn't make Bigfoot or the Loch Ness Monster look blurry in photos, because apparently that doesn't exist already.

A lottery where no one wins. It would be like a real lottery but with one more loser. The benefit of this sort of lottery is that you won't feel jealous that someone else won.

A remote control that screams, "I'm right here," when you yell, *"Where are you?"*

A reverse water filter. It puts germs in the water to help build your immune system.

A placebo pill that does nothing.

A sponge suit that replaces umbrellas. Why waste all that water? Soak it up and use it to mop your floor. Or if you're lazy and vindictive, use it to throw wet sponges at people you don't like.

We already have birdhouses, although I'm not sure why, because birds are perfectly capable of building nests. All we've done by building birdhouses is enable an unmotivated generation of birds so that they never learn construction skills. Also, we've created an inflated market for bird real estate. To help with this problem, I suggest we start making tiny apartment complexes for the birds that can't afford a house yet or have less-than-perfect credit scores.

A trebuchet for her. Trebuchet manufacturers have focused solely on the male market for far too long. It's time for a trebuchet that's current. Trebuchet for her would be pink and have a place to hold a purse along with the boulders. It would also cost more than the original variety because, hey, this is capitalism and apparently women will pay more for the same item in different packaging.

Trebuchet
for her

2 Settings
-Far
-Really Far

Purse Holder
Recycled Wood
Suede Boulder Sack

Precracked eggs. That way you can cook with them without doing the difficult work of slamming them onto the side of the table. Or better yet, let's just have edible eggshells. We may need to change the biological makeup of chickens for this one, but I'm okay with that.

Hopefully manufacturers are hard at work on these things. But if not, I'd just be happy for a QR code on my receipt so I can make my fridge work to its full potential. Because we should all live up to our full potential. And I'm getting tired of having a slacker fridge.

Chapter 10

Car Problems

Like most teens, I bought my first car with the money YouTube gave me. Before you start thinking that I'm conceited and make poor choices with money, let me assure you that I didn't get a fancy new sports car or anything. It was a low-end Mazda that was already a year old.

It was red too.

Every time I drove my Mazda, I kept thinking how crazy it was that I was in a vehicle because people had watched my videos with their ad blocker turned off.

The car was a lot better than the 1997 Buick Park Avenue I'd been driving since high school. My grandparents gave that car to my older sister when she went to college; and it had already been passed down to my cousin Jared; then to my older brother, Luke; and then to Faith and me, who shared it. I guess you could say the car had been around the block a few times—and had the mileage to prove it.

By the time we got the Buick, its teal green paint had more or less completely disintegrated in the Arizona sun, and driving the car felt a little bit like you were steering a boat through traffic. But hey, it was *our* poorly painted boat-car. We drove it everywhere, even though the air-conditioning hadn't worked for years. Riding in it was like getting a free sauna session to and from school every day.

The only benefit to having a total junker car is that when you accidentally scratch the side, your parents don't care that much. I only got a small lecture on responsible driving.

Actually, let me explain how I scratched the car. I worked the closing shift at Sooubway a lot, and the policy was that when employees started the shift, they parked in back of the building. Then, just before closing, we would move our cars to the front parking lot so when we locked up, we would exit the Sooubway through the front door.

One night when I went to move my car, a truck tried to pass me to go around to the back of the store. I edged my car over to the side to let him get by, and I saw that the truck was pulling a trailer full of horses. And it wasn't just a couple of horses. This trailer was towing an entire herd. As you can imagine, this wasn't typical traffic for the back of a Sooubway at nine thirty at night.

I did what anyone in that situation would do: I gawked at the horses as I slowly drove by. And while my focus was on the eight eloquent equines, my car hit a Dumpster and started scraping against it. Even though I was going under five miles an hour, I got a massive scratch that spanned halfway along the side of the car.

I'm still wondering what all those horses were doing in the back of a Sooubway. Maybe it's best not to ask what the mystery meat was made from . . .

Anyway, that's how my car lost even more of its paint.

I wish I could tell you some sentimental stories about the old Buick, but I don't have any. The closest thing to a sentimental moment I had was the time when my mom told me, "Don't plan on living a life of crime, because you'll never be able to use that vehicle as a getaway car." Thanks for always looking out for me, Mom.

I didn't miss the Buick one bit when it finally died. I was driving on a road trip and had just put in a brand-new battery to make sure the car would be able to safely transport me. Was it grateful? No. An hour and a half into the trip, as the Buick was going up an ever-so-slight incline . . .

It couldn't.

So I was pretty happy with my slightly used, one-year-old Mazda because it had only nineteen thousand miles on it, the air-conditioning worked, and all the paint was on the vehicle *and* it was all the same color. At least it was until I accidentally hit my garage door and scraped some off.

Then I heard more about responsible driving, yada yada. My parents couldn't say that much, though, because I was the one who'd bought the car and the garage door wasn't hurt (that much).

After I moved to California and got to experience firsthand the worst traffic imaginable, I decided it was time to buy a car with a backup camera and side sensors to aid me on the battlefield. I bought a second car and gave my little sister the Mazda as a Christmas present. For the sake of this story, we'll call the new car a Sooubaru. It was brand new, beautiful, and still had that new-car smell of whatever they do to cars in factories. We made out constantly.

When my twin sister got married, she had a reception in Arizona a week before Phoenix Fan Fusion, a convention in Arizona I got invited to. I figured instead of having to find people to watch my dog, Floof, for two different occasions, it would be easier if I drove Floof to my parents' house, flew back home after the wedding to get some work done, and then flew to Arizona for Phoenix Fan Fusion. After the conference, I would drive back home to California with Floof.

Floof loves riding in cars, by the way. She thinks it's her job to sit on my lap the entire time and make sure the passing cars don't act suspiciously. She is vigilant about this responsibility.

So my dog and my brand-new Sooubaru were at my parents' house, and the first day I was gone, without mentioning it to me, my dad drove my car to work. (What's wrong with *your* car, Dad?) My car was parked in the driveway behind his car and he figured he would take it to work and fill it up with gas. (Okay, granted, that's a little nice.)

My dad isn't a man of many words—maybe because the rest of us talk so much it's hard for him to get a word in edgewise—but he's always been very good at doing those little tasks that need to be done, like remembering to take out the garbage, pay the bills, and fill up the cars with gas.

Every time he went on long work trips, the rest of the family always forgot to put the garbage out because we're irresponsible.

He contacted building security to see if they had footage of the parking lot and could clearly track down his clearly inconsiderate coworker. Security didn't have that footage. My father works with a bunch of engineers and they're not known for committing crimes in parking lots. My dad went home upset and wondered how he was going to tell me that my brand-new car had been damaged while under his care.

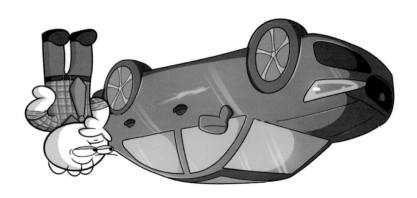

Anyway, after a hard day's work at an unnamed company, Dad was going to drive my car home, when he noticed a scratch on the side of the door. It looked like a white vehicle had sideswiped the Soobaru. He remembered that a white truck had been parked next to him and figured he'd been a victim of a hit-and-run. Or really, a hit-and-drive-off, because obviously the person wasn't running. They had a truck.

The next day he wrote a strongly worded email to the people in the company about owning up to their actions.

Then he walked around the parking lot searching for a white truck that had suspicious blue paint on it. No luck. Engineers are a wily bunch. During his lunch break, he drove the car to a collision repair place to see how much it would cost to have the door repainted.

Keep in mind that it was just a few scratches that were a couple of inches long, not a gaping wound.

The place told him that the car really needed a new door panel and, with labor and parts, it would come to a modest fee of $1,943.

Knowing my dad and his views on responsible driving, he might have paid to have my car fixed and never told me about the incident except that the car place also informed him the repairs would take five days. Although I'm not always really observant, I probably would have noticed if the car had been missing altogether when I came back.

So instead, my father had to come clean. He called me up and said, "James, I have some bad news for you."

I immediately thought that something horrible had happened to Floof, because my dog has no self-preservation instincts.

Actual events that have happened in Floof's life:

Floof eats a black widow spider.

Floof takes on a husky.

Floof has no understanding of traffic.

But instead of saying anything about Floof, Dad began telling me about the car damage.

I said, "Oh, you mean those scratches I got when I accidentally sideswiped a pillar at a gas station? I thought I saw a horse and wasn't paying attention."

Okay, I hadn't actually seen a horse that time. I had no good reason for not paying attention. But at any rate, the scrape had happened not long after I got the car. It turns out that even with all the cameras and sensors, it's still very possible to hit stationary objects.

My dad just hadn't seen the damage when he took the car to work. If he had paid the two grand for my car's repairs, a year or so afterward I might have noticed the door and thought, "Oh, cool, those scratches finally buffed out. I guess they washed away in the rain."

As it was, I ended up being the one who felt bad that he'd been so worried about the damage.

Dad was much happier after our conversation. And then he had to go explain to all his coworkers that none of them were irresponsible hit-and-drive-off jerks. He was just unobservant about the state of the vehicles he drove.

Parenting books probably don't warn people that these are the kinds of situations you sign up for when you decide to have children.

My dad might not think I remember all his lectures on responsibility—and he's right about that. But he's always been a great example of what a responsible person should be like, and that's even more important.

Chapter 11

How We Got Our Second Dog, Poppy

A few months before my sister Faith and I graduated from high school, we noticed that Georgie seemed sadder than usual. She spent a lot of time just lying around moping like this:

Luke had already left home and we started to wonder if Georgie could sense—by that same canine superpower that let Lassie know when Timmy was in trouble—that we would be leaving soon too.

Or maybe we'd all just become so busy with our lives that we weren't paying enough attention to her. We could think of several reasons she might be despondent, and all of them made us feel guilty.

My little sister, who lives by the motto "You can never have enough animals," suggested that getting another pet would make Georgie happy.

"She needs a dog friend to play with her," she kept saying.

The argument did hold some weight, because the one

amazing ability Georgie had was that she somehow always knew when our neighbor's dog, Coco, was at the park near our house. When Coco was out with her owners, Georgie would stand at the window barking hysterically until we finally caved, put her leash on, and took her outside. I'm not sure what our neighbors thought about this. They were probably expecting a quiet game of fetch with Coco, but we kept showing up with our overeager and lonely dog, forcing our neighbors to make small talk with us while our dogs sniffed each other's butts.

Sometimes Coco would race halfway across the park to retrieve a tennis ball, but Georgie had no inkling what the game fetch was about. She would usually just chase after Coco as though she thought Coco might have spotted a stray deer for them to attack (or a Chihuahua—her archnemesis).

Coco didn't mind Georgie dashing along after her, and we became good friends with Coco's owners. But you can only force the neighbors' dog to spend so much time with your dog before you become one of "Those People." Our family was already dangerously close to falling into that category because we had so many cats living in our backyard that it seemed like we were hoarding them. We didn't want to push our luck.

Here's a list of things that make you become one of "Those People":

1. You have a junky, paint-peeling car leaking oil on your driveway.

2. You ask the neighbors if you can put some of your trash in their cans.

3. You make the neighbors' dog have playdates with your dog.

We convinced my mom that Georgie needed to find companionship elsewhere. My little sister began perusing animal shelter websites and showing available dogs to my mom.

ADOPT ME!
·LOVES TO EAT BEES
·HOUSE - BROKEN
·SEX: NO

ADOPT ME! PLEASE
·LOVES KIDS?
·HOUSE - BREAKER
·SEX: ????

And every single one of them was the most adorable thing on the planet.

Finally, one day while my father was away on a business trip, my mother said we could go to a shelter "just to look" at the dogs.

Fun fact: Three out of the four dogs our family has ever owned were acquired while my father was out of town. My dad likes dogs; he just doesn't like the added responsibility.

Anyway, we took Georgie with us because we figured that we would need to know how she got along with any potential candidates while we "just looked" at the available dogs.

Georgie was very excited to go to the shelter because she'd never been stuck in dog jail herself and knew only that it was a place with a lot of very excited dogs behind bars.

The first thing Georgie did to introduce herself to her new potential friends was to poop on the floor. I don't recommend this technique when you meet people. It usually won't have the results you desire, but who knows? Maybe give it a try. A lot of the dogs were large, and we didn't think Georgie would like being knocked out of her alpha-wolf status. After a couple of minutes browsing, we noticed a small fluffy dog in a kennel among the big dogs. Now, I don't mean to use the term "love at first sight" loosely, but it basically looked like this:

Poppy has one talent: looking adorable. On that day, she employed her talent to its fullest.

And it earned her a "Get Out of Dog Jail Free" card.

Actually she was far from free. The shelter charged us almost three hundred dollars. And they say you can't buy happiness.

Georgie seemed to like Poppy well enough, or at least she didn't dislike Poppy, so we thought they would make good friends.

They were fine at the shelter.

And they were fine on the walk to the car.

And they were fine on the car ride home.

But as soon as we brought Poppy inside, Georgie finally clued in that there was another dog in her territory and began barking vigorously at Poppy as though to alert us to her presence in the house.

Again, we never claimed Georgie was a smart dog.

Poppy assured Georgie of her love by repeatedly licking Georgie's mouth, which is a dog pack hierarchy thing that I hadn't known about until we got Poppy.

Poppy was always sweet, loving, and gentle unless Georgie pushed her around too much. Then she would transform, Hulk-like, into this:

This may be the reason why she was placed in the kennel with the big dogs.

She also growled whenever anyone tried to pick her up. This caused problems when she wanted to get up on my bed, since she couldn't make the jump. We actually bought pet stairs so that the dogs could just walk up onto my bed by themselves. Unfortunately, neither of the dogs was smart enough to figure out how to use them (even though we have stairs in our house) and we ended up returning them. (The stairs—not the dogs.)

We'd asked the lady at the shelter if Poppy was house-trained. The lady said they didn't know because Poppy was a stray. We soon learned that no, Poppy was definitely not.

We made sure to take Poppy outside a lot, and every time she went to the bathroom, we rewarded her with a treat. To this day, every time she goes outside, she thinks we should give her some food. Sometimes she goes outside, sits on the patio for three seconds, and then turns around to come back inside and expects us to give her cheese.

How hard is it for a dog to go to the bathroom? When we go for walks, Poppy apparently needs to relieve herself every five feet, but at home she will refuse to go to the bathroom for hours.

While we were working on potty-training Poppy, we noticed that Georgie was going to the bathroom a lot. At first we thought she was being helpful and wanted to show Poppy how the whole using-the-lawn-as-a-bathroom worked. But nah, that's not what it was. Georgie kept having to go more and more—and then we realized that some of the inside accidents were coming from Georgie, not Poppy.

We took Georgie to the vet and found out that she had bladder stones and needed a $2,600 surgery. It turned out that earlier when she'd been lying around and acting despondent, she hadn't been lonely or contemplating us leaving home. She'd just been sick.

And so that's how we spent a lot of money to remove Georgie's bladder stones and also got stuck with another dog. But we love Poppy, and despite her anger issues, she and Georgie were great friends, so that worked out pretty well.

After Georgie's surgery, she went back to her normal, happy self. I'm not sure how sad she was when Faith and I left for college, but she and Poppy certainly were happy whenever we came back.

Chapter 12

Proof the World Is Flat

In this chapter, I'll give you definitive proof that the world is flat. After many diligent hours of research on the internet, I have finally found absolute proof that the world is not a globe. Pay attention to these next few pages, as I'll go into great depth about how the government has lied to you.

Listen, I know I'm basically saying that for this theory to be true, most of the population has to be wrong. But it wouldn't be the first time. After all, people used to think that the Earth was the center of the universe, and they wore bell-bottom jeans. (Not at the same time, probably.) So, to prove that the Earth is flat, all you'll need to do is get thirteen thousand

HOW TO PROVE THE WO
STEP 1
FLY TO
ANTARCTICA

STEP 2
DRAW THIS
SYMBOL
IN THE
SNOW:

S
D
DR

and you'll find the results as stunning as I have. Since this is a very important chapter, the Illuminati might try and hide this knowledge from you. You have to be careful of the Illuminati. They could be anyone from anywhere: your teachers, your dentist, or even your publisher! But I don't think they'll do any tampering with this book. I mean, all I did was give out a well-guarded government secret. What are they gonna do? Not print the pages? Pft.

In the next chapter, I'll give you proof that the moon landing was faked.

Chapter 14

The Missing Mattress

**Discussion questions for your book club
(should you ever have a book club)**

1. While reading this chapter, think about the struggles the author had to go through to get his mattress back. Ask yourself if this is what being an adult is like.

2. When is it appropriate to say, "Let me speak to your manager"?

3. Have you ever misplaced someone's mattress? If so, *how?*

Generally, I'm not a "Let me speak to your manager" type of person. That's because I realize that people wearing tacky fast-food uniforms have very little choice about working at their minimum-wage jobs. I don't get mad when my food takes too long or when the ice-cream machine is broken.

Not everyone is as understanding. Some people feel entitled because of propaganda like the phrase "The Customer Is Always Right." In my experience, the customer is *almost* always wrong. How long have you been working here, customer? I've been here for over a year. I know what I'm doing.

So I almost never get mad at employees.

Sometimes, however, you *should* turn into one of those difficult customers and demand your money back. This, unfortunately, is part of being an adult. Not a part you look forward to, like driving, buying spray paint, and having politicians pander to you. No, this is a part of adulthood like the moment when you realize you'll have to buy your own groceries for the rest of your life.

What I thought my life as an adult would be like:

What it's actually like:

Recently something happened with a business that got on my nerves. I didn't pull the "Let me speak to your manager" card, but I could feel my inner–mom instincts kicking in and telling me, "You should threaten to give them a one-star review on Yelp!"

My apartment lease ended on the tenth of the month and I was moving into a house on the fourteenth. Since I didn't want to pay a bunch of money to extend the lease for an extra month, I hired a moving company to take all my furniture and put it in storage, which meant that I would technically be homeless for four days. Here's my advice to anyone who's thinking about being homeless: Don't do it.

When it was the fourteenth and I got to sleep in my house, I had nothing but Floof, an air mattress, and the shirt on my back (I lost my pants). I always keep an air mattress in my trunk in case of emergencies. Learned that my first day on the streets. Of course, an air mattress is only helpful in emergencies when I also have access to an outlet, because I have to plug in the mattress to inflate it.

That first night in my house, I got to experience what it's like to be a minimalist, but I'm not going to lie, I still felt like I was homeless.

Anyway, the movers called me and said they would deliver my furniture on the fifteenth, between seven and nine a.m.

I said, "Sounds good," and set my alarm to eight o'clock, thinking that, statistically, I would be fine.

Floof woke me up with her barking at seven o'clock when the movers arrived.

After the men had been unpacking their truck for a while, I felt weird standing around not helping them so I decided to make small talk.

"How much more stuff do you guys have?" I asked one of the movers.

"All that's left is the couch and the armchair," he said.

"And my mattress, right?" I asked.

The man looked puzzled. "Uh . . . no. There's no mattress in the truck."

These same movers had carted my bed away less than a week before. They'd brought in and put together my bed frame, but somehow they didn't think it was strange that there wasn't anything to put on top of it.

SLEEPING HABITS OF CALIFORNIANS

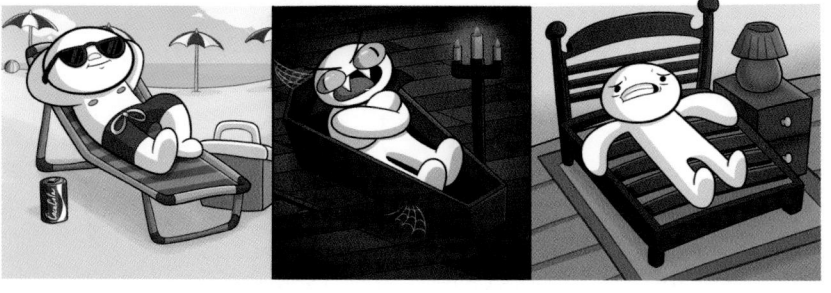

I didn't worry that much because I figured the movers must have my mattress somewhere. It's kinda hard to misplace bed-size objects. And it's not like my mattress could've run off. I made sure to cut off his legs as soon as I bought him.

I thought I would just have to make *one* phone call to customer service, and the moving company would find my mattress in the storage unit or hiding underneath someone's bed and they would deliver it without any problem.

But instead, customer service told me to fill out a damaged or missing items claim on their website. The movers had taken pictures of everything they put into my storage unit, so they should have had all my items in a database. I looked through those pictures, though, and my mattress had never been documented. As far as the movers knew, I owned a bed frame without a mattress.

YOUTUBERS ARE WEIRD...

I figured that since my (ex-)roommate moved out on the same day and used the same movers, the movers must have accidentally put my mattress in his unit. He was getting his furniture delivered a couple days later, so I texted him about my predicament and made sure to use plenty of emojis so he knew how serious the situation was.

That night as I slowly nodded off to sleep, I dreamed about seeing my mattress again and the many comfortable nights soon to come.

In the morning, I called customer service again and told the receptionist my theory. She looked into my roommate's account and asked, "Can you describe the mattress in a way that confirms it belongs to you?"

Usually I'm very good about describing mattresses, but

for some reason this time I drew a blank. What did she expect me to say—"It lies around and answers to 'Mattress'"? Instead, I said, "Can you just tell me if there are two mattresses in his unit? Because I know for a fact my roommate only uses one mattress."

She said, "I'm sorry, I can't disclose that information."

What?! Why not? It was a *mattress*. I wasn't asking for his social security number.

So I did my best to describe the mattress. "It's rectangular shaped and has some pee stains on it." I should've clarified they were from my dog. I don't have that problem anymore.

The receptionist said, "Oh, actually I do see a mattress that fits that description. If it's yours, we'll move it to your account."

Problem solved . . . probably.

When my old roommate finally called, I asked him to check his inventory to see if my mattress ran off with his.

He sent me his inventory pictures and he had only one mattress listed. I knew it was his because it had his social security number burned on the side.

I hoped the reason he only had one mattress was that the company had caught and corrected their mistake.

Day 2 on the couch.
My mattress never showed up in my account. My roommate got his stuff delivered that day, but the movers didn't have a second mattress on their truck.

"Where's my mattress? Did it fall off the truck? Did the lady lie about seeing it in the first place? Does she even work for

the moving company? What was her name again? Denise? What did you do to my mattress, Denise? Are you trying to sabotage my sleeping schedule? Where is my boy?"

I called customer service again, and calmly and sleep-deprivedly told them everything that had happened. The unconcerned person said I needed to fill out a form and asked me to provide a picture of the missing item.

I looked on my nightstand for the framed picture of my mattress that I usually keep with the picture of my vacuum cleaner and my toaster, but I couldn't find it anywhere. I guess the movers lost that too.

I googled "mattress with black trim" and used a picture of a $3,000 mattress. Because, hey, maybe I would get lucky and they'd find a better mattress for me.

I wanted to add to the missing-item report: "I won't rest until I get that mattress, because I need it to sleep."

After I submitted the form, I got an email saying:

> Your claim is currently being reviewed by an agent who will work with you to resolve this as quickly as possible. You can expect to hear from your claims agent within 2 business days.

Problem was, it was *Saturday*. The business days don't start counting down until Monday.

Day 4 on the couch.

I decided that every night I had to sleep on my couch, my review of the moving company would go down one star.

Around two p.m. on Monday after not hearing from my agent, I got impatient and called customer service for the fourth time. The receptionist told me there were no new updates on Matty the missing mattress.

I heard the words form in my brain. I could've said them right then. Just six little words and all my problems could be fixed.

"Let me speak . . ."

I couldn't bring myself to do it. So instead I passive-aggressively wrote a chapter in this book.

When this sort of thing happens to me, my friends never give me any sympathy. After I told them about my AWOL furniture problem, they all said, "But it's great material for a video."

Sometimes I don't want material. Sometimes I want to sleep on a bed.

As I was complaining to one of my friends, she said, "James, aren't you going to have a guest room in your new house?"

"Yeah," I said.

"Won't you need to buy furniture for it?"

"Yeah," I agreed.

"Why not just buy the guest bed now?"

And that is why you need friends—to point out obvious solutions to you. I'm a little embarrassed how many nights I slept on that couch. I went to a mattress store that day and bought a brand-new bed for the guest room. They delivered it to me the same day and I finally got a good night's sleep.

So technically I was my own guest.

It took the moving company a whole week to find and deliver my mattress. I don't know where Matty was, or what happened on his adventure, but he came back with a passport, a suntan, and passable Spanish.

And then to add insult to injury, the moving company had the audacity to email me asking for a review. Thanks for reminding me.

Sometimes doing the adult stuff isn't easy. It involves making phone calls, talking to strangers, and filling out forms—none of which I enjoy. In this case, I did everything wrong, except for listening to my friends.

Chapter 15

Things I'm Supposed to Like but Don't

Society expects everyone to like certain things, but some of those things don't exactly tickle my fancy, if you know what I mean. I guess you could call me the odd one out. (I make these jokes because I care about you.)

Granted, there are people who take pride in not liking something to the point where it becomes toxic.

OH YOU LIKE THAT TV SHOW?? WELL AS AN INDIVIDUAL WITH AN ABOVE AVERAGE IQ, I ONLY WATCH SILENT FRENCH FILMS.

THAT'S TRUE ART.

A person who thinks this way feels that they have more refined tastes than the average person's and are therefore above the status quo. I like to call these people "hipsters." They need to learn to let the average person enjoy average, pathetic things.

What I'm trying to say is that I don't mean to come off as an elitist. Since this is a list of popular things I dislike, many of you will think I'm wrong. That's fine. I'm not trying to change your opinion, I'm just trying to write something you'll find entertaining.

If you're feeling concerned that I'm about to start bashing things that you enjoy, here are some things that I like that you also like:

- Puppies

- Reading a book that a YouTuber wrote

- Macaroni and cheese

- The lights aisle at Home Depot

- Cracking your back

- Going to the bathroom after holding it in for a while

- Some TV shows

But not all TV shows. One TV show I'm not a fan of is this show called *Football*. This show has been going on for fifty-four seasons, and honestly, I don't see the appeal. Episodes are repetitive, the writing is confusing, the cinematography is flat, there are too many characters to keep track of, and I can't relate to any of their struggles. Also, for some reason, they all want to hold this oddly shaped ball. I must have missed the episode where they explained why it's so important.

Football episodes always have a huge live studio audience at the tapings. The audience is so big that a lot of times they can be seen in the shots—which I wouldn't mind if the audience wasn't screaming every time the show started to get interesting. Whenever *Football* airs the season finale, I get invited to viewing parties and people cosplay as their favorite character. I always go because of the free food, but I'm never caught up in the show, so it's hard for me to get invested. Oh well, at least the commercials are entertaining.

Because of the success of the show, it's spawned a huge number of spin-off shows.

FOOTBALL ON ICE

TALL FOOTBALL

FOOTBALL WITH A STICK

HANDLESS FOOTBALL

Now that I'm thinking about it, in *Handless Football* the characters use their feet more than the characters in plain *Football*, so calling this show *Football* and naming the original *Football* something else would make a whole lot of sense. What if instead we made an acronym to describe handless football. How about: Society Of Cool, Constantly Energetic Runners. S.O.C.C.E.R.

I've had plenty of people tell me, "James, *Football* isn't a fictional narrative with plots and characters. Those aren't actors; they're professional athletes playing a sport."

But that just got me thinking about the word "sport."

Speaking of sports cars, I'm not sure why some car models are called sports cars. As far as I can tell, none of these cars are involved in playoffs or can hit a ball in any direction. Unless your car happens to run over a S.O.C.C.E.R. ball. Not that I've ever done that. At least not that I'm going to tell you about.

Most guys my age like sports cars because they have flashy high-tech features. They make sounds like "zoom" and "ka-chow" and "nnyyooooommm." They can go from zero to sixty miles an hour in negative-two seconds. Maybe I'd be impressed with those numbers if I drove on an airport runway and could actually go that fast. But no. I live in California, where traffic moves a little faster than your average ice-cream truck full of open glasses of milk.

Sports cars are also super expensive. In fact, despite their horsepower, they're much more expensive than a horse and they love you less. Using horses might be slow, but at least you'll get good gas mileage. A sports car costs approximately the equivalent of a college education or 123,000 sticks of butter.

(YOUR BUTTER STACK MAY VARY DEPENDING ON THE SPORTS CAR)

I think I'm just not into that rich-boy lifestyle. What's the point of paying more for something just so that people know you paid more for it?

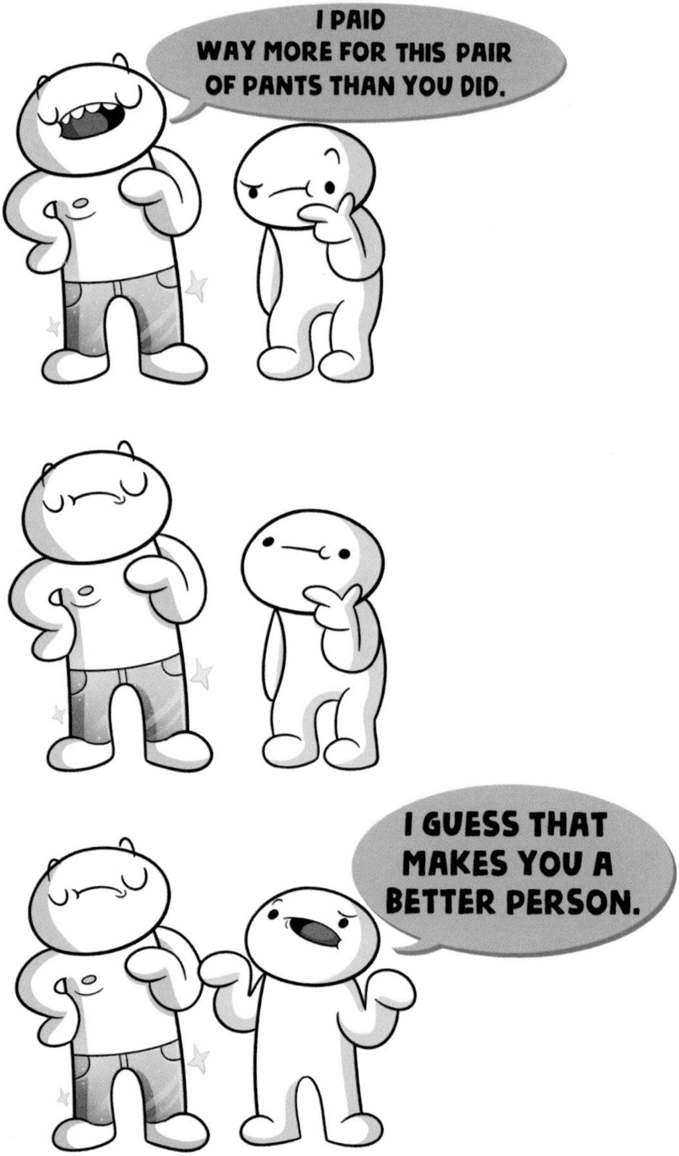
I PAID WAY MORE FOR THIS PAIR OF PANTS THAN YOU DID.
I GUESS THAT MAKES YOU A BETTER PERSON.

Not only do some people buy unnecessarily expensive clothes, they also expect the rest of us to wear outfits where our shirts match with our pants. I don't know who made these rules or why we let them dictate fashion, but apparently you're not supposed to wear two different patterns, and your colors are supposed to coordinate. Unless you're wearing jeans. If you wear jeans, you can wear any color and we all pretend it matches with navy blue.

I think I talked about how I don't understand fashion in my first book, but I'm very passionate about these feelings.

The thing about me, though, is that I don't want to wear any clothes that are less comfortable than pajamas. As soon as I put on a pair of pants, I think about how long it will be until I can take them off again.

If you've been agreeing with everything I've said thus far, don't worry, you're really going to change your mind when I say that I'm not a fan of stories in video games.

The first video game I ever played on my parents' old Macintosh was Lode Runner. In the game, you're a robber trying to steal money bags all while these cops you can out-run chase you. Also you have the power to make holes in the ground by pressing the A button, and if a cop happens to fall into your hole, you can walk over him. Just like in real life.

Lode Runner had all the story a game needs: Steal bags of money and run so fast you don't get caught. The game had a hundred different levels but I could never get past level 6. Luckily I knew the cheat code that let me skip any level.

I was perfectly content with that lifestyle. Because when I play a game, I want to *play the game.* I don't want to watch an unskippable cutscene and then be told, "Now, go here to watch another cutscene. *Hey, idiot, pay attention to this cutscene because there's going to be symbols flashing on the screen and if you don't press the corresponding button fast enough your character will die and you'll have to watch this cutscene again!"*

Maybe someday I'll play a video game that changes my mind, but right now I think that all the story a video game needs is: Go save the princess. And that's the exact story to one of the highest-selling video game franchises:

Shrek.

Last on the list of things I'm supposed to like but don't is literally every book I was forced to read in my high school English classes. People complain a lot about being forced to take math. You always hear them say stuff like, "When am I ever going to use the Pythagorean theorem *in real life?*"

Do you know how many times I've used my knowledge of the symbolism in *The Scarlet Letter?* Never.

Which is a good thing because I did not retain anything that was in that book.

In ninth grade, I had to read *Walden* by Henry David Thoreau, and it was the most boring book ever. No action, no saving princesses. It was all about philosophy and living in nature. Thoreau obviously didn't live in Arizona or he wouldn't have had a pond to write about and living off the land would have been a lot harder.

"WATER..."
BY HENRY DAVID THOREAU

"I DON'T NEED ANYTHING ELSE."

Fun fact: While he was living in the cabin, people from the city brought him food, and his mom did his laundry. If I went to live by a pond, I'm pretty sure my mom would not do my laundry.

I recently decided to give one of the classics another try, so I read *Lord of the Flies* (because I lie to myself that I'm the sort of person who can appreciate mid-twentieth-century British allegorical fiction). The book is basically a commentary on human nature. And granted, anyone who's ever been shopping on Black Friday may wonder how quickly people can revert to savages, but I really think the author had an unnecessarily pessimistic view of people. The schoolboys get along for a little bit, but then two characters get in a fight and almost immediately this group of twelve-year-old schoolboys are painting their faces, decapitating wild pigs, and killing each other.

When I was a scout, I went camping in remote woods with other twelve-year-old boys all the time. Sure, our scoutmaster was there, but we never fought, unless we were pulling pranks on each other, or unless one boy had some candy and I wanted it, or unless we played "the stick game," where we had to push each other out of a circle drawn on the ground, or unless a friend and I filled up a ziplock bag full of water and threw it on top of some kid's lean-to, or if there was any body of water—then we would all try to push each other in no matter how shallow it was.

Okay, maybe *Lord of the Flies* isn't completely inaccurate.

There are probably more things that I dislike and you don't, but I won't go over all of them. People don't have to like the same things to be friends. This isn't junior high. (Unless you are in junior high, and then this *is* junior high.)

Be as individual as you want. It's okay to be unique. And it's okay to change your mind about what you like. So go ahead and try new things. You don't always have to go with the flow. The important thing is that you . . . wear your seat belt.

Acknowledgments

I will now acknowledge this book. This is indeed a book that definitely exists. Whether it's good or bad is completely up to you, dear reader. But you did read it all the way to the end, and you're reading the acknowledgments too, so I hope that's a sign you did enjoy it.

As this book comes to a close, I just want to thank you so much for reading it, and let me know in the comments if you think I should make another one.

Also thanks to all the additional artists that worked on this book: Jordan Miller, Kat Herrera, Annie Loomis, Pantless Pajamas, Ed Nielsen, Alise Veilande, Tom Martin, and Hiro the Hiroshark.

Thanks to my agent, Tim Travaglini, for constantly calling me to ask if the book was done yet. I appreciate that, Tim.

Thanks to my editor, Lauren Appleton, even though she told me to take out a few jokes. Probably a good call. And thanks to the whole publishing team at TarcherPerigee.

And thanks to my mom, who keeps trying to teach me correct English.

About the Author

James Rallison has been drawing comics since he was eight years old. This would be an impressive fact if the comics had been good, but they were just the average sort of eight-year-old drawings. Fortunately, he persisted with his artwork, or this wouldn't be a very good book. (It is.)

At age sixteen, James created the webcomic *The Odd Is Out*, which has expanded into a YouTube channel with millions of subscribers. He lives in California with his loyal dog, Floof. So many other people also live there that rocket scientists are currently working on ways to solve the traffic problem.

Also by James Rallison

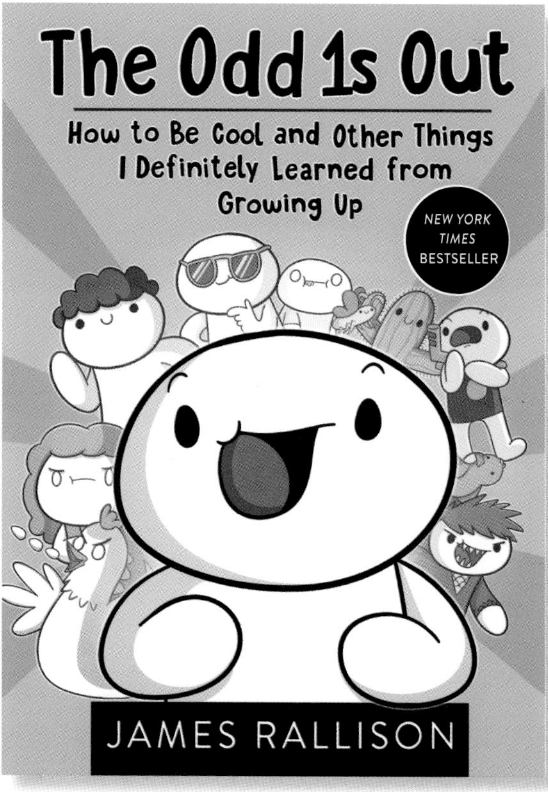
The Odd 1s Out
How to Be Cool and Other Things I Definitely Learned from Growing Up
NEW YORK TIMES BESTSELLER
JAMES RALLISON